M000038906

ESPECIALLY FOR

FROM

DATE

SECRETS OF
HAPPINESS

Inspiring Thoughts for a
More Joyful You

SECRETS OF HAPPINESS

Inspiring Thoughts for a
More Joyful You

MICHELLE MEDLOCK ADAMS

BARBOUR
PUBLISHING

Published by Barbour Publishing, Inc., P.O. Box 719, Uhrichsville, Ohio 44683, www.barbourbooks.com

Our mission is to publish and distribute inspirational products offering exceptional value and biblical encouragement to the masses.

Member of the
Evangelical Christian
Publishers Association

Printed in China.

"These things I have spoken to you, that My joy may remain in you, and that your joy may be full."

JOHN 15:11 NKJV

In memory of my father,
Walter Medlock, and for my mother,
Marion, who both taught me the secret to
real happiness—a relationship with Jesus.
I love you!

CONTENTS

IGNORE THE BUZZARDS

*Don't you realize that in a race
everyone runs, but only one person
gets the prize? So run to win!*
1 Corinthians 9:24 NLT

I was just finishing the second-to-last lap of my three-mile jog—and definitely feeling the pain. Every pore in my body was sweating profusely. My face was red, and I was huffing and puffing quite loudly. It had been a few days since I'd run, and my body seemed to scream, "Hey, what are you doing? You're hurting me! Quit working so hard!"

Pushing through the pain for the final lap, I noticed a big ol' buzzard circling overhead. I had to laugh. It was as if that buzzard was waiting for me to keel over. (I guess I must have looked even worse than I felt.) But I was just stubborn enough to run the last lap even harder than I had run the previous eleven. That buzzard wasn't about to discourage me from achieving my goal.

Have you noticed any buzzards circling lately? They come in many forms—negative bosses, disapproving mothers, critical friends—you name it. A "buzzard" is anyone or anything that comes to squash your dreams, steal your happiness, and tell you that you are not good enough. For some people, it was growing up in a home with negative parents. For others, it is a husband or boyfriend who never encourages them. Or maybe it is a friend who is always ready to offer a little dig that makes you feel less than capable.

No matter what form your buzzards take, be

assured they will come. But you have to learn to ignore them. Block them out and press forward. Run your race, and encourage yourself in the Lord.

We read in the Bible that David had to encourage himself. He and his men had just returned home from a daunting battle to find their camp ravaged. Their wives and children had been captured by enemies, and their camp had been burned. David could feel the buzzards circling—especially when his men turned on him and talked of stoning him.

But David didn't give in to his sadness. The Bible says that he encouraged himself in the Lord. And guess what? Just seventy-two hours later, David and his men had regained their families and belongings, and David was named king.

Buzzards, schmuzzards. If you are feeling overwhelmed by those buzzards circling overhead, just encourage yourself in the Lord. Keep pressing toward your goals, and hang on to your happiness. Just think what might happen in seventy-two hours.

● ● ●

PINK PROMISES

*I am sure that nothing can
separate us from God's love—
not life or death, not angels or spirits,
not the present or the future.*
ROMANS 8:38 CEV

After my father died, my sister and I helped our mom go through his personal items. I couldn't wait to get into Daddy's special drawer—it was the one drawer in his nightstand that he kept off-limits to us kids. I remember once trying to ease open the drawer to sneak some quarters from his big bowl of change (I wanted to feed the Pac-Man game at the local arcade), but as I started to reach my hand inside, I heard Dad's voice: "Michelle Leigh Medlock, get out of my drawer!" He didn't mind giving me money for Pac-Man; he just didn't want me in his special drawer.

For years I wondered what could possibly be in that forbidden treasure trove. Why was he so protective of it? Now I would finally know. As I searched through Daddy's things, I found very ordinary items. His comb. Fingernail clippers. His money clip. Pictures of the family. Lots of change. His special calculator he used in business. And a lockbox. When we opened it, we found important documents like his and my mother's marriage license, birth certificates, and the hospital bracelets for all three of us kids—two tiny pink ones and one small blue one. The wording had yellowed over the years, but I could still read "Medlock Girl" and my birth date on one. I held that tiny pink bracelet close to my heart for what seemed like hours.

At that moment, I realized how very much my daddy cherished me. He loved me so much that he even treasured my baby bracelet. Today I keep that baby bracelet in a secret compartment of my purse as a reminder of how much Daddy cared.

You may not have a loving earthly father. Or maybe you don't even know your father. But I have good news: You have a heavenly Father who treasures you, and He has little pink bracelets—His promises of love—all throughout His Word. Every time you find one (like Jeremiah 31:3, which says, "I have loved you with an everlasting love"), you will want to hold it close to your heart—just like I did. Spend some time discovering how much your heavenly Father loves you today. It will fill your heart with real joy that will last a lifetime.

PEACOCKS OF HAPPINESS

*You, LORD God, have done
many wonderful things,
and you have planned
marvelous things for us.
No one is like you! I would never be
able to tell all you have done.*
PSALM 40:5 CEV

Hurrying into the office one afternoon, I was totally focused on an upcoming meeting. I was going over some mental notes when, all of a sudden, I looked up to see the most beautiful sight. Next to the front door of our office building stood a brilliant blue peacock grooming himself in the sun. Rays of sunlight bounced off his fabulous feathers, making the sight even more breathtaking. I literally stopped in my high heels, for a moment experiencing total joy. I wanted to squeal like a little girl on Christmas morning. I just couldn't believe my eyes!

No, I hadn't been sniffing my pink highlighter. There really was a peacock outside, which I later learned belonged to a nearby rancher. This beautiful bird liked to roam, and on this particular day, he had roamed right into my life.

As I stopped to appreciate the peacock's beauty, I thanked God for reminding me of His presence in the midst of my day—showing me love and favor even when I'm caught up in the busyness of life.

The day had started like any other, but right in the middle of the mundane, God had dropped a peacock of happiness into my morning. While later contemplating my surprise visitation, I realized that God drops "peacocks of happiness" into our lives all the time. Unfortunately, we are often too busy or our hearts too hardened to notice.

You may never have a fantastic feathered friend show up outside your home or office, but be on the lookout for God's good work and loving-kindness toward you every day. Be mindful of Him all day long, and drink in those moments of pure joy. Maybe your peacock of happiness will come in the form of your child's laughter. Or maybe your peacock will be the lovely fragrance of a honeysuckle bush. However your peacocks come, take time to enjoy them, and praise the Lord for His blessing. God loves to surprise us with good things—especially when we appreciate the "peacocks" He sends into our lives.

YOU CAN'T
BUY HAPPINESS

This is how we know what love is:
Jesus Christ laid down his life for us.
And we ought to lay down our
lives for our brothers and sisters.
If anyone has material possessions
and sees a brother or sister in need
but has no pity on them, how can the
love of God be in that person? Dear
children, let us not love with words or
speech but with actions and in truth.

1 John 3:16–18

According to an article in *USA Today*, you can't buy happiness—no matter how rich you become. In fact, University of Illinois psychologist Ed Diener was quoted in the story as saying, "Materialism is toxic for happiness."

So, contrary to popular belief, buying an entire collection of Jimmy Choo shoes will not make one happy. Now, I have to be honest with you: I love to shop. When I walk into a department store, my heart pounds with excitement. Sale racks full of designer clothing beckon me. Flashy handbags and sterling silver jewelry seem to dance under the store's fluorescent lighting, making a smile spread across my face. I truly enjoy shopping, so when I read this article, a part of me said, *Well, these people just don't know where to shop. I could show them happiness if they'd come to Dallas.*

But, in reality, that kind of happiness is fleeting.

Do you know why? Because true happiness doesn't come from acquiring things for oneself; true happiness comes from giving to others.

I am not saying that shopping is a bad thing. I am, however, saying that Jesus' words "It is more blessed to give than to receive" (Acts 20:35) are true. God created us to be givers because we are made in His image, and He is the greatest giver of all. He gave His one and only Son to die on a cross so that we could have eternal life with Him. As Christians, the desire to give should be strong in us, too.

If you have felt unfulfilled and less than happy lately, look at your own generosity. Have you become a taker more than a giver? When is the last time you looked forward to placing a tithe in the offering plate? Have you recently done anything totally unselfish for someone else? If it has been too long, then get back into the giving mode.

Call that frazzled single mom in your neighborhood and offer to watch her children for a while. Invite that widower in your church over for dinner and fellowship. Buy school supplies for an underprivileged child. And do it all unto the Lord. You will find that giving is the greatest high—even better than discovering Jimmy Choo shoes on sale!

IS YOUR GLASS
HALF FULL?

*Rejoice always, pray without ceasing,
in everything give thanks; for this is
the will of God in Christ Jesus for you.*
1 THESSALONIANS 5:16–18 NKJV

Are you a glass-half-empty or a glass-half-full person?

You might say that's a foolish question because, either way, it's just half a glass. Quantitatively, that's true. What you think doesn't increase or decrease the actual amount of liquid in the glass. But *qualitatively* it makes a huge difference—between an unhappy or a happy existence.

A few years ago, the media company I worked for experienced a difficult financial year. As the holidays approached, we received a memo that read, "Due to our challenging financial year, we are unable to give you, our treasured employees, Christmas bonuses this holiday season." The letter continued with a heartfelt apology, a plea for patience, and a prayer for a better new year.

When the infamous memo arrived on our desks, the glass-half-empty people were livid! To be honest, we glass-half-full folks weren't exactly doing the dance of Christmas joy, either—but the difference between the two groups' reactions was vast.

The glass-half-empty employees griped for months. If they were asked to do anything beyond the norm, they would grudgingly comply—then say something sarcastic like, "Yeah, we'd be happy to get right on that because our company has done so much for us lately." The glass-half-full folks, on the other hand, continued to work hard and hope for a better future.

The following December, we received another envelope on our desks, but this time it didn't contain just a memo. It held a memo and a Christmas bonus check. Sighs of relief and whoops of celebration rang out in the glass-half-full camp. Guess what the glass-half-empty group did?

They complained.

"Well, it's about time!" was heard from certain cubicles. Or, "Better late than never!" or "Too little too late, if you ask me."

It was a good lesson—one I'll never forget. I saw firsthand how glass-half-empty folks and glass-half-full people handle life's day-to-day ups and downs. The bottom line? I discovered that glass-half-full people live happier, fuller lives than the glass-half-empty folks. When faced with exactly the same circumstances, one group chose to be happy and the other depressed.

So I ask you again: Are you a glass-half-empty person or a glass-half-full person? If your glass looks half empty today, fill up on God and change your perspective. The level in your glass may not change, but your level of happiness will!

YOU'RE NOT TOO OLD!

*"For I know the plans
I have for you," says the* Lord.
*"They are plans for good
and not for disaster,
to give you a future and a hope."*
Jeremiah 29:11 nlt

Do you have regrets? Do you sometimes feel like the best part of your life is already over? That can be the cause of intense unhappiness and dissatisfaction. In fact, several studies have revealed that the older a person gets, the more likely it is that that person will become depressed. It seems old age and depression go hand in hand.

But they don't have to!

All of us have dreams we have never realized, but here's good news: It is never too late. No matter what your age, you are not too old to fulfill the plans God has for your life. The parade hasn't passed you by. You haven't missed the boat. You are not too old!

Did you know that Grandma Moses started painting at age seventy-six? Without any art classes or special training, she painted simple, realistic pictures of rural settings—paintings of historic importance.

Look at Sarah in the Bible. She didn't have her son of promise—Isaac—until she was long past the natural childbearing age. Sarah had given up on having her own child, but God hadn't. He was happy to fulfill her dream and to use Sarah to bring Isaac into the world.

So what dream has God placed inside you? Is it to write a book? To teach a Bible study? To start your own business? Now let me ask you this: What's holding you back? In Jeremiah 29:11, God said He had good plans for His people. Don't you think He has a good plan for you?

Stop regretting and instead rekindle that dream inside you. Ask God to bring it forth in His perfect time. If you feel like you're too old, ask God to change your perception of yourself. He wants you to realize your dreams because He's the One who put them there.

Jesus came to give you a full life. But you have to want it, too! Spend some time today meditating on your dreams—even those you have let go of—and commit to praying over them until they are realized. That faithfulness in itself will bring happiness and hope.

GOD IS A GOOD GOD

Give thanks to the Lord,
for he is good;
his love endures forever.
PSALM 107:1

Some days it's harder to be happy than others. Whether it's hormones or atmospheric disturbances or a lack of sunshine, there are days when I feel a heaviness of spirit before my feet even hit the floor. On those days, I know Special K cereal and OJ just aren't going to cut it. Mornings like that call for the breakfast of champions—Diet Coke and a Snickers. Can you relate?

On those difficult mornings, I have to choose to be happy—so I start by thinking on good things. I choose to meditate on the goodness of God. And it works!

Think about all the times God has come through for you. Think about the many blessings He has given you. Think about His ultimate sacrifice—sending Jesus, His only Son, to die on a cross just so you and I could be saved. He is such a good God!

But sometimes it's not enough just to *think* about God's goodness. Some days you need to declare His goodness out loud. Sure, it might seem weird at first, but just try it. Say, "God is so good to me!" Say it several times a day. Then add, "I am the apple of God's eye. He cherishes me and highly favors me."

Next, try quoting some verses about God's goodness. Psalm 107 is a good place to start. Say, "Give thanks to the LORD, for he is good; his love endures forever!" If you are into singing, you can add a chorus of "God is so good." (Remember that powerful little chorus from church camp or vacation Bible school?)

It's a fact: You can't meditate on the goodness of God and be unhappy at the same time. So the next time you're having a "blue Monday" or a "foggy Friday," turn your thoughts off yourself and onto the goodness of God.

Make a conscious decision to choose happiness today, tomorrow, and the next day, and celebrate the goodness of God. That's the best way to start the day—even better than Diet Coke and a Snickers!

WHERE ARE YOU LOOKING?

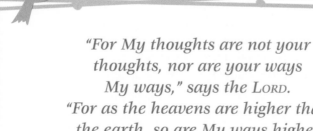

*"For My thoughts are not your
thoughts, nor are your ways
My ways," says the LORD.
"For as the heavens are higher than
the earth, so are My ways higher
than your ways, and My thoughts
than your thoughts."*
ISAIAH 55:8–9 NKJV

Helen Keller used to say, "When one door of happiness closes, another opens; but often we look so long at the closed door that we do not see the one which has opened for us."

Most everyone has read the story of Helen Keller. She was born a healthy, happy child in Tuscumbia, Alabama, on June 27, 1880. But at the age of nineteen months, she suddenly lost her hearing and vision as a result of illness—possibly scarlet fever. Her life was forever changed. She was forced to grow up in a hearing and seeing world she didn't understand, one that didn't always embrace her.

Her story is one of great persistence and triumph over adversity. Beating overwhelming odds, this highly intelligent, sensitive woman devoted her life to bettering those around her.

You might say she chose to look for the open doors.

Let me ask you this: Are you looking for the open doors in your life? When one door closes, do you stand there staring at it, longing to batter it down? Or do you trust God for another door of happiness?

The Word tells us that God's ways are higher than our ways and His thoughts are higher than our thoughts (Isaiah 55:9). In other words, He may close a door that you're sure is the only one that will ever lead to happiness. You may plead with Him, "Please! Open the door!" And all the while, He is trying to get your eyes back on Him so He can show you the even better door of happiness that He has waiting for you.

So don't waste any more time staring at the closed doors in your life. Get your eyes back on God and let Him show you that next door of happiness. It may be right in front of you.

BE JOYFUL,
NO MATTER WHAT!

Rejoice in the Lord always.
I will say it again: Rejoice!
PHILIPPIANS 4:4

In Paul's letter to the church at Philippi, he mentions *joy* or *rejoicing* more than a dozen times. What makes that so amazing is this: Paul was in prison when he wrote Philippians. And it wasn't just any old jail. Greek scholar Rick Renner studied the historic details of the prison where Paul was held and recently shared those findings with our church. It seems that this Roman prison was known as one of the worst in the entire empire.

The prison had actually been used as a septic pit for many years and over time had evolved into a lockup for the worst offenders. Prisoners were chained with their arms above their heads and forced to stand in human waste up to their hips. The prisoners had to stand at all times—no matter how weary they became. Since the prison had no windows or ventilation, the smell must have been horrid. In fact, many prisoners died from toxic fumes. Others died from rat bites and infection. Still others died from hopelessness.

The prison was *that* bad—so awful it sucked life itself out of many strong men.

So how could the great apostle write about rejoicing in the Lord? Paul had learned that the source of his joy had nothing to do with his environment or his physical state. He found his joy in Jesus Christ. It was God's own Son who enabled Paul to write: "Rejoice in the Lord always. I will say it again: Rejoice!"

Paul was surrounded by darkness, dung, and doom—but his heart was full of Jesus and joy. He fixed his eyes on eternal things. Paul knew that the Lord was with him in his suffering, and he knew that Jesus would deliver him from that place of despair.

So how is your joy level today? Take a lesson from the apostle Paul—rejoice no matter what! God is with you. He loves you, and He's completely aware of your situation. Don't be moved by your circumstances—even if you are waist-deep in debt, sickness, marital problems, physical addictions, or whatever. God is able to deliver you. So rejoice in the Lord always—again I say, rejoice!

LET THE PAST BE THE PAST AT LAST

*Forgetting what is behind and
straining toward what is ahead,
I press on toward the goal to win the
prize for which God has called me
heavenward in Christ Jesus.*
PHILIPPIANS 3:13–14

Ralph Waldo Emerson wrote: "Finish each day and be done with it. You have done what you could; some blunders and absurdities have crept in; forget them as soon as you can. Tomorrow is a new day; you will begin it serenely and with too high a spirit to be encumbered with your old nonsense."

In other words, "Get over it! Move on! Tomorrow is another day!"

Okay, so you totally messed up yesterday. Maybe you yelled at your children, ate too many Twinkies, acted disrespectfully to your employer, or spoke sharply to your spouse. Whatever you did wrong yesterday, be quick to repent and move on.

The devil will try to make you dwell on your past mistakes, but you don't have to go there. Once you have asked for forgiveness—both from those people you offended and from Jesus Christ—you're good to go! You get to start the next day with a clean slate. God doesn't remember the mistakes you have confessed, so why should you? Don't let yesterday's blunders steal today's joy.

Remember, guilt and condemnation are not from the Father. So if you are experiencing those emotions, realize their origin—they come from the devil. He wants you to feel so badly about yourself that you will never move forward. Know why? Because the devil understands the awesome plans God has for your life, and he doesn't want you to enjoy your bright future. The enemy will do anything he can to keep you in your past, so don't fall for his tricks.

Instead, learn from your mistakes and move on. Let the past be the past at last! Praise the Lord for His unending mercy and love, and ask Him to help you become more like Him. You are a work in progress. We are all like spiritual babies, learning to walk and occasionally falling down—and that's okay. Quit glancing back at your blunders; keep your eyes on Jesus. Your future is happy and bright in Him.

WORKING ON A GREAT TESTIMONY

We know that God is always at work for the good of everyone who loves him.
ROMANS 8:28 CEV

Have you ever heard the expression, "Without a great test, you can't have a great testimony"?

I'd have to say "Amen" to that truth.

When I began this journey as a writer, I received enough rejection letters to wallpaper my entire office. Now, even after I've had more than twenty books published, the rejection letters still come. Rejection is simply part of the publishing world.

A few years ago, my friend Gena and I signed a contract for our compilation for women called *Divine Stories of the Yahweh Sisterhood*. We were very excited about the project. We had worked on it for more than six months, signed a contract with a well-known Christian publisher, and met our copy deadline.

Several weeks after submitting the final draft, we still hadn't heard from our publisher. Nor had we received a copy of the signed contract for our records. Instead, we got a telephone call, letting us know that the publisher had experienced a tough fiscal year and was forced to hand back several contracts—including ours.

We were stunned.

The test had begun.

Determined to find another publisher, we began submitting to every publishing house we thought might be interested. We even hired an agent to represent the book for us, but nothing happened. No one seemed to want our book.

"But God. . ."

Say that out loud right now: "But God." When God steps in, things transpire in ways you never could have imagined. Though we were unsuccessful in our search for a publisher, God had it all worked out—in His perfect timing. He supernaturally connected us with a wonderful publisher in 2005, and the book was released in January 2006—selling more than twenty thousand copies in its first week of release. That was a miracle, and it was because God stepped in and took over. His favor has continued to make a way for our book.

But it was definitely a test for Gena and me. We had to keep our hearts right and believe that God had called us to write that book—that He would finish what He had started by publishing it. And that's just what happened. Now we have a testimony that encourages other writers to hang on to their dreams.

If God has given you a dream—no matter what it is—hang on! Don't fail the test, because the testimony will be so sweet! Keep saying, "But God," and keep your heart full of joy. Your testimony is on the way.

LONELINESS AND HAPPINESS DON'T MIX

God has said, "Never will I leave you;
never will I forsake you."
HEBREWS 13:5

Mother Teresa once said, "The most terrible poverty is loneliness and the feeling of being unloved."

If you're feeling lonely today, happiness may seem far off. Loneliness has a way of consuming your life, leaving little room for anything else—especially happiness. You may be alone due to circumstances beyond your control. Maybe your spouse came home one day and simply said, "I don't love you anymore," leaving you and the life you had made together. Or maybe your spouse died and now you're trying to build a new life on your own. Or maybe a recent move left all your friends behind. Or maybe you're in a great marriage and surrounded by friends—yet you still feel lonely.

It happens.

Whatever your situation, God understands and cares. He wants you to know that you are never alone—no matter how lonely you might feel at this moment. He promises in His Word never to leave you nor forsake you. That's great to know, isn't it? God is right there with you, loving you through your good and bad times.

God wants you to escape the loneliness you're feeling and embrace the joy He has to offer. Sure, that's easier said than done, but you can take a step away from loneliness and toward happiness right now. Here's how: Get your focus off yourself and meet someone else's needs today. Seek out a single mom in your congregation and offer to babysit for her. Or visit some of the shut-ins from your church—they'd love to have a friendly visitor. Or get involved in your church's hospital and prison ministries, and make a difference in the life of someone less fortunate than you.

The devil wants to keep you in your own isolated little world. But don't let him. Leave your comfort zone and reach out and touch someone with the love of Jesus today. The sooner you start helping others, the sooner your loneliness will be replaced with purpose and joy.

JEALOUSY IS
A JOY STEALER

It's healthy to be content,
but envy can eat you up.
PROVERBS 14:30 CEV

English Quaker leader and founder of Pennsylvania, William Penn, wrote, "The jealous are troublesome to others but a torment to themselves."

Jealous people are some of the unhappiest people in the whole world. Even when good things happen to them, they are too consumed with ill feelings to enjoy their blessings. Instead, they focus on people who have more than they do—and feel cheated instead of grateful.

Sure, we call jealousy cute things like "that old green-eyed monster," but in reality, the feeling is demonic. It originated with Lucifer himself. Many Bible scholars agree that Lucifer's rebellion against God was motivated by jealousy.

Jealousy is serious. It is the opposite of love. Undealt with, it ultimately leads to murder. In fact, jealousy is what led to the very first homicide in the Bible—Cain killing his brother Abel.

So jealousy does a lot more than simply steal your joy. It can steal an entire life—yours or that of someone else. Don't play around with jealousy. When that green-eyed monster first rears its ugly head, smash it! Don't allow jealousy to linger in your heart even for a minute. Instead, face jealousy head-on and destroy it.

Here's how to do it: Pray for the person you are most jealous of, and go out of your way to show that person kindness. Yes, you will probably have to do it by faith (and maybe through gritted teeth), but do it anyway. Every time you pray for that person, you are smashing that old green-eyed monster right between the eyes. Every time you compliment the person who makes you most jealous, you are choosing love over jealousy—and ultimately, happiness over turmoil.

One other thing: Read the Love Chapter (1 Corinthians 13) every single day, and read it this way, "I am patient, I am kind. . . . I do not envy. . . ." Before long, you will have so much love in your heart, there won't be room for jealousy.

MAKE THINGS RIGHT

*"This is how I want you to conduct
yourself in these matters. If you enter
your place of worship and, about
to make an offering, you suddenly
remember a grudge a friend has
against you, abandon your offering,
leave immediately, go to this friend
and make things right. Then and
only then, come back and work
things out with God."*
MATTHEW 5:23–24 MSG

At times, all relationships can be challenging. Whether a friend, family member, coworker, or boss has fallen out of your good graces (or you have fallen out of theirs), don't you think it's time to make up?

People stay mad at one another for years—so long, in fact, that they can't even remember why they were mad in the first place. Still, they keep the anger torch burning year after year. Ridiculous, isn't it? Maybe so, but it's a reality for many people.

Is it a reality for you? If so, your happiness level is probably depleted. Broken relationships are definitely joy stealers. They weigh heavily on your mind and heart, but they don't have to anymore. You have the power to change that today.

If your mother always treated a sibling better than you and you have held a grudge against your mom for years, call her today. She may not even know that you have felt angry and hurt all this time. Simply say, "Mom, I've been mad at you for far too long, and I'm sorry. I love you and I want to put the past behind us." If calling seems too scary, send her a card.

This plan is a good one no matter whom you need to reconcile with—your mother, father, coworker, sibling, grandparent, ex-spouse, child, or someone else. Even if the person you contact doesn't reciprocate your kindness or want to restore the relationship, you have done your part. The burden is off of you, and you can move on.

If the person you are angry with has already passed on, write that person a letter. Write all the things you wish you had said while he or she was alive. After you have written the letter, pray over it. Say, "Lord, I give this over to You. I repent for holding anger in my heart for so long, and I put that anger and hurt under the blood of Jesus right now."

This brings us to the most important relationship of all—the one we have with Jesus. If you have been mad at God over something, repent and restore that relationship today. He loves you, and He has a good plan for you. Reconciliation is the first step to restoring your happiness. Take that step today.

DON'T GIVE UP!

*"Be strong. Take heart.
Payday is coming!"*
2 Chronicles 15:7 MSG

Chip Brim, a sports enthusiast and minister of the gospel, once shared a vision he'd had. The Lord showed him thousands of Christians running down a football field. They started off strong, running with all their might, striving toward a touchdown. But when they reached the one-yard line, they fell to the ground. Not one of them made it across the goal line to make that all-important score. Instead, they all perished right there—one yard from their destiny.

Why? What happened? Chip wondered. God impressed on his heart, *They gave up too soon. They threw in the towel. They didn't know how close they were.*

Sad, isn't it? How many of us start out strong, running as hard and as fast as we can toward that end zone, yet never cross the goal line?

Too many of us.

Let's face it. Life is difficult at times. It's hard to stay in the game. It's hard to keep trying. It's much easier to give up. But giving up will never bring ultimate happiness. So you have to hang in there—no matter how hard it gets.

Harriet Beecher Stowe said, "When you get into a tight place and everything goes against you, till it seems as though you could not hold on a minute longer, never give up then, for that is just the place and time that the tide will turn."

Well, the tide is turning for you. Just hang on. Ask God to help you see the goal line. Ask Him to help you continue running toward the destiny He has for you—no matter how difficult your race becomes. He wants you to cross that goal line even more than you do. It breaks His heart to see His children throwing in the towel so easily, because He knows that their happiness resides in His perfect will for their lives—on the other side of that goal line.

If you have fallen down on the one-yard line, get back up. Ask God to help you. He will do His part, but you must do yours. Keep pressing toward your dreams. Pretty soon you will be doing the "dance of joy" in the end zone.

SPREAD THE JOY!

Love is kind.
1 CORINTHIANS 13:4

Every single day we encounter joy stealers. You know the type—rude cashiers, angry drivers, inconsiderate coworkers, and even grouchy family members. You'll have an opportunity (probably before breakfast) to get mad, but you can choose kindness instead.

Not long ago I encountered one of those joy stealers at the supermarket. This cashier was angry. I don't know why—maybe she'd had a fight with her husband before work, or maybe her boss had just given her crummy hours for the next week. Whatever the cause, this gal was not in a good mood. As she scanned my items, she was muttering under her breath. Though I hated to disturb her, I had a few coupons to use, which I slid toward her.

Glaring at me, she snapped, "You're supposed to hand those to me at the beginning of the transaction."

Ever been there?

Now, what I wanted to say was, "Listen, sister, I'll report your rudeness to your supervisor. Don't push me."

But my heart wouldn't let me. Instead, I answered, "Oh, I'm sorry. I wasn't aware of that policy. If it's too much trouble, I can just save them and use them the next time I go grocery shopping."

She didn't even respond, so I continued.

"I bet you get tired of rule breakers like me, eh?"

She cracked a smile.

"Some days it's an aggravating job," she shared in

a much nicer tone.

"Well, I don't envy you," I added. "I used to work retail for a clothing store, and I know how the public can be. Some days I just wanted to scream."

"You've got that right," she chimed in.

Before she scanned my last can of green beans, we were best buddies. She not only let me use my coupons, but she gave me a couple of extra ones she had at her station.

We chatted a bit more while she bagged my groceries, and then I told her to keep up the good work and try not to let the aggravation get to her. She smiled a full-out smile and said, "I'll try not to. . .and you come back and see me."

I didn't let this cashier steal my joy. Instead, I gave her some of mine. You can do the same. Joy is contagious. Be a carrier and spread it everywhere you go.

MIRROR, MIRROR

*I praise you because of the
wonderful way you created me.
Everything you do is marvelous!*
PSALM 139:14 CEV

How do you see yourself? Do you have a negative perception? When you look in the mirror, do you see a child of the Most High King, or do you focus on your flaws? If you're like most people, you probably see the imperfections.

Women, especially, struggle with self-esteem. Spend any length of time around a group of women, and before long, you will hear a conversation something like this:

"Back in the day, I had it going on," one woman will say. "But now everything has shifted—and not in a good way."

"I hear you," another will add. "I lost fifteen pounds last year and regained twenty this year. I just tell everyone I'm like Garfield the cat—fluffy, not fat."

The gals will giggle and joke, but many of those same women are hurting inside. They feel so badly about themselves that they don't enjoy life. Are you one of those hurting people?

If so, let me encourage you today. I'm right there with you. I am certainly not perfect—inside or outside. Every year I find it harder to fit into the latest fashions, and "the barn needs a little more paint" before I leave the house. If I let myself, I could dwell on every single flaw I have, but I choose not to go there. You shouldn't, either.

Instead, ask God to help you see yourself as He

sees you. God thinks you're amazing. He doesn't mind if your thighs aren't model thin or your hair is a bit on the frizzy side. He thinks you're wonderful, and He wants you to think you're wonderful, too.

Remember that old saying, "God doesn't make any junk?" Well, it's as true today as when we learned it in vacation Bible school. You are priceless. You are far more precious than rubies. You have got it going on in God's eyes. After all, He created you!

Let God's love shine big in you, and forget about those size 6 jeans that no longer fit. Sure, it's okay to work on your outer appearance, but don't let that consume you. Let God's love overwhelm you and spill out onto all the people around you. Get up every day, look in the mirror, and say, "I may not be perfect, but I am perfectly loved." Starting each day with that confession will put you on the road to happiness—even if you're having a bad hair day. Just grab a cute hat and greet the world with love and happiness in your heart.

DON'T WORRY, BE HAPPY

*"Can any one of you by worrying
add a single hour to your life?"*
MATTHEW 6:27

Remember that '80s song "Don't Worry, Be Happy"? (You're singing along right now, aren't you?) Well, it's not only a fun song with a great reggae beat, but it's also good advice. "Don't worry, be happy" is a good motto to adopt, because worry will steal your joy faster than you can say "leg warmers."

Worry is a sneaky thing. You might start the day just thinking about a situation in your life, but if you think too long, you will end up in full-out worry mode. You will start thinking things like, *If those layoffs really happen at our company, I don't know what we'll do. We just barely make it now. What if I can't get another job with health insurance? What if I don't get a severance package? What if? What if? What if?*

Don't let your thoughts take you there. If you cross over into the land of worry, you will eventually drive into the territory of fear and ultimately hit the city limits of despair. It's not worth it! Besides, no matter how much you worry, it doesn't change the situation one single bit, right? Prayer is what changes things.

Worry is not only a happiness stealer, it's a sin. The Bible instructs us not to worry. Matthew 6:34 says, "Therefore do not worry about tomorrow, for tomorrow will worry about itself. Each day has enough trouble of its own."

That's pretty clear, isn't it?

Worry is a hard habit to break, especially if you have lived your whole life as a worrywart. But it's not impossible to overcome. How do I know? I was a world-class worrier for many years. I'd think about something for a while and eventually work myself into such a tizzy that I wanted to hide under the covers and eat bonbons all day. Ever been there?

If you have been taking regular trips to the land of worry, get off that highway. Take the prayer detour and stay on that road until you reach your final destination of peace, happiness, and victory. And while you're "in the car," pop in an '80s CD and sing along with "Don't Worry, Be Happy." Good tunes always make the journey more fun!

HOPE AND HAPPINESS GO HAND IN HAND

Jesus looked at them and said, "With man this is impossible, but with God all things are possible."
Matthew 19:26

Hopelessness.

If you have ever experienced it, you know how awful it feels. Hopelessness sucks you dry of any joy, peace, or victory in your life. In fact, it can be suffocating, stealing the Word from your heart and blanketing you with heaviness. When hopelessness sets up camp inside, it leaves no room for happiness. (Maybe that's where the expression "not a happy camper" came from?) Bottom line: Hopelessness is not of God.

Actually, Satan is the king of hopelessness. He loves to get out his big old magnifying glass for you to look through. He will show you all the problems in your life and whisper, "Look how big they are! Your problems are beyond fixing. They are too big for God." But let me tell you something: Satan is also the father of all lies. So if he tells you that your problems are too big for God, you can boldly say, "Liar, liar, pants on fire!" Nothing is impossible for God.

You may have lost your hope today, but I have good news: You can get your hope back right now. Maybe you're saying, "But, Michelle, you can't fix my problem"—and you're right, I can't. But I know Someone who can.

Not only can our heavenly Father fix your problems, but He is eager to do so. You, however, have to do your part. You have to get your faith on. You have to believe that He is able to do all things, and then stand on that promise whenever Satan whispers lies into your ears. You have to believe that God is able to come through for you—no matter how bad the circumstances. Do you believe?

Pray this right now:

> *Lord, I am feeling hopeless today.*
> *I am overwhelmed with the problems*
> *in my life, but I know that You are able*
> *to do all things. And I am asking You*
> *to intervene on my behalf. I praise You*
> *today for the victories that are yet to*
> *come. Please remove the hopelessness*
> *from my heart and replace it with*
> *supernatural happiness. Let my life*
> *bring glory and honor to You and*
> *encourage those around me. Amen.*

Okay, it's a done deal. God is working behind the scenes at this very minute on your behalf. Hang on to your hope, and happiness is sure to come.

THERE IS NO "I" IN TEAM

You can easily enough see how this kind of thing works by looking no further than your own body. Your body has many parts—limbs, organs, cells—but no matter how many parts you can name, you're still one body. It's exactly the same with Christ.
1 CORINTHIANS 12:12 MSG

Is your nickname "Tammy Takeover"? Do you try to do everything alone? If so, we should form a support group—because I also struggle with that I'll-just-do-it-myself attitude.

Of course, that line of thinking isn't original. The world has been telling us for years, "If you want something done right, you have to do it yourself." So I decided I would. I tried to do it all—all by myself—all the time. I ended up overwrought, stressed, and mean. (Yes, just ask my husband. I *so* didn't have the joy of the Lord in my life.)

God didn't intend for us to go it alone. He even addresses that errant line of thinking in 1 Corinthians 12:12, using the human body as an example of teamwork. We are just one part of the big picture. We each play an important role, but we will never accomplish what God has for us if we try to do everything all alone. Why? Look to the verse for the answer: According to God's Word, we are just one part of the body. No matter what a great eyeball you are, you will never be able to hear, because you're not an ear!

So quit trying to be an ear! Be the best eyeball you can be, and work with the person in your life who was called to be an ear. Together, you will do much! Alone, you will just be a good eye—nothing more.

Teamwork, whether you are in an office setting or helping with vacation Bible school, is vitally important.

Lose the "Tammy Takeover" mentality and do your part with the rest of the body, and big things can be accomplished in a short time. And the really great part is that you will be much happier! You will get to enjoy the experience and celebrate with the team members when "all of y'all" (Texan plural for "y'all") meet your goal! It's a win/win situation.

So go out and do your part, but don't try to do everyone else's part, too. If you feel yourself moving into the I-can-do-it-all-by-myself mode, ask God to keep you focused on what He has called you to do and nothing more. Remember, there is no "I" in TEAM—but there are great rewards and happiness when we choose to work as a team.

GET OUT OF THE CAR

*"Now have come the salvation
and the power and the kingdom of
our God, and the authority of his
Messiah. For the accuser of our
brothers and sisters, who accuses
them before our God day and night,
has been hurled down."*
REVELATION 12:10

Have you taken any guilt trips lately?

If you answered yes, then it's time to get out of the car. Guilt is not from God. The Bible tells us that the devil—not the Lord—is the accuser of God's children. God sent Jesus to die on the cross so that we could be free.

Free is free.

The freedom that Jesus bought includes freedom from eternal damnation; freedom from fear; freedom from lack; and freedom from condemnation and guilt. You don't have to take guilt trips if you have asked Jesus to be the Lord of your life.

But the devil will still try to lure you into his car and take you on a long, depressing road trip. He loves to remind you of all the mistakes you have made. He loves to tell you that God could never love you because you have been such a bad person. He is the chauffeur of all guilt trips, ready to take you on an extended drive whenever you will let him.

Don't let him. Just get out of the car!

Maybe you're saying, "But you don't know how badly I've messed up my life. I deserve guilt. I deserve to be unhappy."

If you really feel that way, then you have fallen for the devil's lies. I want to remind you of the truth: If you have asked Jesus to forgive your sins and be Lord over your life, you are guaranteed eternal life and His joy. (If you haven't, please pray the prayer at the end of this entry, and we'll take care of that right now.)

The next time the devil whispers in your ear, "You don't deserve happiness because you have done too many bad things in your life," boldly answer: "I am saved. Jesus wiped away all my sins and removed them as far as the east is from the west. He no longer remembers my sins, so why should I?"

That's what the Word says—and using the Word of God against the devil is your best defense. Just say no to guilt trips. Remind the devil that you are on the road to heaven—and he can't make that trip with you.

PRAYER OF SALVATION

Heavenly Father, I come to You in the name of Jesus. Your Word says that everyone who calls on the name of the Lord will be saved [Acts 2:21], and I am calling on You right now. I ask You, Jesus, to come into my heart and be the Lord of my life. Now, according to Romans 10:9, which says, "If you declare with your mouth, 'Jesus is Lord,' and believe in your heart that God raised him from the dead, you will be saved," I say that Jesus is Lord and that I believe He was raised from the dead and now resides in my heart. I praise You, God, that I am a Christian. Amen.

FIND YOUR PRECEDENT

Elkanah made love to his wife Hannah, and the Lord remembered her. So in the course of time Hannah became pregnant and gave birth to a son. She named him Samuel, saying, "Because I asked the Lord for him."
1 Samuel 1:19–20

The Bible is more than just a good book filled with great stories. It's alive. It's pertinent. It's full of promises. It's our lifeline! So why do so many of us leave it on the coffee table instead of discovering its power and relevance today?

My oldest niece, Mandy, found out just how powerful and alive the Word of God is when she began believing for a baby. She and her husband, Chris, tried for several years to conceive, but every month the pregnancy test came back negative. She was discouraged. Lots of people gave her advice: "Take this vitamin, and it will help you get pregnant"; "Try conceiving when there is a full moon"; "Stop eating acidic food and you'll have a greater chance of success." Mandy followed every bit of advice, trying desperately to become pregnant—but the only thing she became was depressed.

Then her mother suggested, "Mandy, honey, why don't you find some scriptures to stand on? Find your promises in the Word of God and pray them over yourself every single day. The Word works!"

Mandy had been a Christian since she was a little girl, so she was certainly open to the suggestion. Since that was about the only thing she hadn't tried, Mandy was willing to give the Word a shot. She dug into the Bible and found the story of how Sarah had given birth to Isaac. Then she found the story of how

Hannah had believed God for a baby and finally given birth to Samuel and several other children, too.

Mandy found a precedent in the Word of God and asked God to do for her what He had done for Sarah and Hannah. And He did! She stood on those scriptures for three months, and that's when her pregnancy test came back positive. Mandy gave birth to a healthy baby boy on February 15, 2006.

Jesus once told a story of an oppressed widow who pestered a judge until she got the justice she so desperately wanted. The moral of the story? According to Jesus, people "should always pray and not give up" (Luke 18:1).

Not every prayer will be answered the way we may hope. Even Jesus asked His Father if the trauma of the crucifixion could be avoided—but concluded His prayer with the words "yet not my will, but yours be done" (Luke 22:42).

God has promises for all of us—promises of an abundant life and of peace, hope, and joy. Those universal promises may also include personal blessings for our families, workplaces, and churches. So dust off that Bible and find what God says about your situation. The Word works all the time. Now, that's something to be happy about!

HOLD ON FOR YOUR MIRACLE

While Jesus was still speaking, some people came from the house of Jairus, the synagogue ruler. "Your daughter is dead," they said. "Why bother the teacher anymore?" Overhearing what they said, Jesus told him, "Don't be afraid; just believe."
MARK 5:35–36

Sometimes when you are holding on for a miracle, your situation gets worse. Actually, you can almost count on it getting worse. This pattern occurs often in the Bible.

Look at Jairus, the synagogue ruler. His daughter was very sick—at the point of death. He had heard about Jesus and knew that Jesus was capable of healing his girl, so he went to Jesus and said, "My little daughter is dying. Please come and put your hands on her so she will be healed and live" (Mark 5:23). Jesus began to go with him, and as He pressed through the crowd, the woman with an issue of blood received her healing by touching the hem of Jesus' garment.

As all of this transpired, Jairus was still waiting for Jesus to come to his home and heal his daughter. But then some men arrived from Jairus's house and said, "Your daughter is dead. Why bother the teacher any more?"

Jairus's situation definitely got worse, didn't it? Think about it. He sought out Jesus for his sick daughter because she needed a miracle. While Jairus was waiting his daughter's miracle to happen, the woman with an issue of blood received her miracle. Then men from his house came with news that his daughter had already passed away.

What was Jesus' response? He said, "Don't be afraid; just believe."

At that point, Jairus had a decision to make: *Do I go with fear or faith?* Had he chosen fear, Jairus would have buried his daughter. But he chose faith. He chose to follow Jesus' instruction and believe, and instead of burying his daughter, he made her dinner that night. She was totally healed!

See, it doesn't matter how bad your situation seems. It doesn't matter if you receive the worst possible news. It doesn't matter if you have been holding on for a miracle and now your situation has gone from bad to worse. Jesus is saying to you, "Don't fear; only believe."

If you will choose faith over fear, you will experience a much happier and more victorious life. So choose faith today—and hold on for that miracle.

LIVE TO GIVE

*Remember that our Lord Jesus said,
"More blessings come from giving
than from receiving."*
ACTS 20:35 CEV

My pastor recently preached a sermon titled "Live to Give." I jotted down those three simple words in my Bible, and I underlined them with pink highlighter for extra emphasis. Why? Because I never want to forget the importance of having a giving heart.

My daughters have certainly adopted this lifestyle of giving, and it thrills my soul. At Christmastime, they can hardly wait to take a tag from the Angel Tree in the foyer of our church. They love buying presents for children who might not otherwise receive gifts.

Last year, my thirteen-year-old, Abby, chose an angel tag that listed the wishes of a three-year-old girl. We were asked to purchase two items from the list, but Abby didn't want to stop there. Using her own birthday money, she went down the list of desires and purchased each item. From Dora the Explorer pajamas to Elmo house slippers—Abby made sure that every wish on that little girl's list was fulfilled.

Abby discovered firsthand that giving really is better than receiving.

How long has it been since you flowed in the "live to give" mode of operation? How long has it been since you did something nice for someone without expecting anything in return? If you can't remember, then it has been too long.

Don't wait until Christmas to adopt a giving attitude—start today! Ask your pastor if you can buy school supplies for some of the financially challenged children in your church. Or purchase some diapers and bless that new single mom in your congregation. Chances are, she needs all the help she can get.

Giving doesn't have to be monetary, so don't feel badly if you don't have extra cash. You can give your time to a worthy cause, such as a local soup kitchen, a nursing home ministry, the local humane society, your church nursery—whatever. Chances are, most any organization would be thrilled to have your help.

Ask God to give you opportunities to sow into the lives of others every single day, and He will. Soon you will discover the joy of giving—and you will be as happy as a three-year-old girl in new Dora the Explorer jammies!

REST IS BEST

*By the seventh day God had finished
the work he had been doing; so on
the seventh day he rested from all his
work. Then God blessed the seventh
day and made it holy, because on
it he rested from all the work of
creating that he had done.*
GENESIS 2:2–3

Most people would agree that the Ten Commandments are very important. Even non-Christians can rattle off four or five of them, right? So why is it that we sort of skip over the one that tells us to keep the Sabbath day holy (see Exodus 20:9–11)? It is clearly one of the "Big Ten," yet we rarely treat the Sabbath any differently from other days of the week.

Interestingly, "Remember the Sabbath day by keeping it holy" is really the oldest commandment of them all, being around since the very beginning. When God created the world, He did it in six days, then rested on the seventh. He didn't rest because He was tired (God doesn't get tired); He did it as an example for us. He knew that we workaholics would work seven days a week if given the chance, and He also knew that such a schedule would be detrimental to our spiritual, mental, and physical health.

So why do many of us continue to stress ourselves by working seven days a week? Are we afraid we won't succeed if we don't work every single minute? If you fall into that workaholic category, take a lesson from a very wise businessman—S. Truett Cathy, the founder of Chick-fil-A.

A committed Christian, Cathy has always honored the Sabbath day. From the very beginning, he established a six-day business week—closing all of his restaurants on Sunday. Sounds like a bad business decision, doesn't it? But Cathy and Chick-fil-A have never suffered from it. In fact, he did a study of his Chick-fil-A stores in shopping malls and discovered that his restaurants made more money in six days than the other fast-food chains made in seven days.

God's principles work—and He will always honor those who honor His Word.

So quit killing yourself with nonstop work. Honor God on the Sabbath. Spend time with Him. Spend time with your family. Spend time resting yourself and getting ready for the week ahead. If you will do things God's way, you will live a much happier and healthier life.

YOU'RE QUALIFIED

But Moses said to God, "Who am I that I should go to Pharaoh and bring the Israelites out of Egypt?"
EXODUS 3:11

I recently read a bumper sticker that said, "God doesn't call the qualified; He qualifies the called."

That's good, isn't it?

In a world that demands qualifications for just about everything, isn't it nice that God demands only our willingness to serve Him? In fact, God calls imperfect people.

Look at Moses. God had a huge job for him in spite of the fact that Moses had killed an Egyptian, hid him in the sand, and then fled Egypt because he was afraid of what would happen to him.

Not exactly a glowing résumé, is it?

Besides that, Moses had a speech problem—yet God was asking him to approach Pharaoh and tell him to let God's people go free. Moses knew he wasn't qualified. In fact, he said to God, "I have never been eloquent, neither in the past nor since you have spoken to your servant. I am slow of speech and tongue" (Exodus 4:10).

But the Lord already knew that, and He still wanted Moses for the job. He said to Moses, "Who gave human beings their mouths? Who makes them deaf or mute? Who gives them sight or makes them blind? Is it not I, the LORD? Now go; I will help you speak and will teach you what to say" (Exodus 4:11–12). God already knew that Moses wasn't a gifted orator. He already knew all of Moses' shortcomings, but He still chose

Moses to lead the people of Israel out of Egypt into the Promised Land.

Guess what? God knows all of your shortcomings, too—and He doesn't care. He wants to use you anyway. God doesn't need your qualifications or abilities. He just wants your willing heart and availability. He will take care of the rest.

So trust Him today and be encouraged. You are qualified in God's eyes. You can be excited and happy about your life because God has a plan and it's a good one (see Jeremiah 29:11). You may not feel qualified to do the things God has called you to do, but God is more than qualified—and He's got your back!

TALK YOURSELF HAPPY

*"For by your words you will
be acquitted, and by your
words you will be condemned."*
MATTHEW 12:37

How's your talk? Are you speaking things that agree with the Word of God, or are you talking negatively about yourself and your circumstances? If you are using your mouth to say negative things, then you have little hope of having a happy, positive, and fulfilling life.

Your words are very powerful. You can do a lot of damage with the words you speak—not only to people around you, but to yourself.

Bible teacher Darlene Bishop wrote a book titled *Your Life Follows Your Words*. In it she talks about the importance of speaking only what the Word says about you. Instead of saying, "I am so broke; I'll never be able to pay my bills," say, "My Father owns the cattle on a thousand hills. He supplies all my needs." Instead of saying, "I am so stupid; I can't do anything right," say, "I have the mind of Christ. I can do all things through Christ who gives me strength."

Darlene didn't originate this idea; it's a biblical principle. Proverbs 18:21 says, "The tongue has the power of life and death, and those who love it will eat its fruit."

So take a moment today to listen to yourself. If the words coming out of your mouth are negative and contrary to God's Word, then change your talk. Begin thinking on God's Word, memorizing God's Word, talking God's Word, and acting on God's Word.

That's the secret to a happy life. Get your mouth right, and your life will soon follow.

PRESS 1 FOR GOD

Be constant in prayer.
ROMANS 12:12 AMP

When my father was alive, I phoned him every single morning. I loved hearing his voice. I loved listening to his stories. But more than anything, I loved the way he listened to me. He always had time for my silly stories, my meanderings, my questions. He always had time for me.

I missed Dad so much after he died. Even now there are still mornings when I reach for the phone, momentarily forgetting that he has moved on to heaven. One morning, crying out to God and telling Him how much I missed my dad and our talks, I heard that still, small voice say, *"You can talk to Me."*

It was at that moment I realized that I had been so close with my earthly father that I hadn't spent much time speaking to my heavenly Father. Typically, I only prayed when I needed something. I rarely talked to God about the day-to-day stuff.

That morning was a turning point for me. I began talking to God just like I'd talked to my earthly dad. I didn't wait for tragedy to strike before calling on God. Instead, I started talking to Him about everything.

You know what I discovered? God is a great listener, too. You will never get His answering machine, and He always has time to listen to you. Isn't that good news? You can talk to God about anything, and He longs for you to converse with Him.

The Lord wants to be more than just a "big God in

the sky." He wants to have a close relationship with you, but you have to allow Him into your life. He is a gentleman who won't force His way into your day. Why not include Him today?

Share your hopes, dreams, fears—everything—with Him. And make sure you spend time listening for His still, small voice. He has much wisdom and insight to share with you.

As you spend more time talking with the Lord, you will find that there is much happiness in Him. Go ahead and talk to God right now. You have a direct line!

YOUR SEASON OF HAPPINESS IS AHEAD

There is a time for everything. . .
a time to weep and a time to laugh,
a time to mourn and a time to dance.
ECCLESIASTES 3:1, 4

Life has different seasons. Some are happy and exciting. Some are difficult and challenging. And some are filled with tears and sadness.

When my best friend lost her first baby—a little boy—I didn't know how she and her husband would survive such a loss. But God knew. He was right there with them as they dealt with the overwhelming grief. They found refuge in the Father's arms. Today they have two beautiful little girls, but there are still times when my friend longs for the baby boy she never had the opportunity to know. On those days she runs to the Father's arms and lets Him comfort her aching heart.

Maybe you have suffered a devastating loss and are wondering if you will ever escape this season of grief and sadness. Maybe you are right in the middle of a sad situation, and there are days when all you can do is cry. Or maybe your pain has continued for many years and you can't seem to get rid of the hurt in your heart.

Whatever your situation, God cares. The Bible says He records our tears (Psalm 56:8); in other words, the Father knows every tear you have ever cried. He loves you so much that He hurts when you hurt.

You can turn to Him when you're having a hard day. You don't have to put on your brave face with the Father. He knows what is in your heart anyway, so be honest with Him. Tell Him about your hurts, fears, sorrows, and desires. You can crawl up into your heavenly Father's lap any time of the day or night and let Him comfort you.

No matter how much you are hurting right now, know that sadness is only for a season. Ask God to mend your broken heart and infuse your soul with joy. He will. And He will lead you into a season of happiness. There is a time for everything. Isn't it time for you to be happy?

FRIENDS BRING HAPPINESS

*Friends love through
all kinds of weather.*
PROVERBS 17:17 MSG

Friends.

Television shows, hit songs, and countless stories have focused on the special people we call friends. Special occasions such as "Friendship Week" and "Best Friend Day" have even been established to honor them. Why? Because friends are important.

Friends are there for us in good times and bad. They support us when we need a shoulder to cry on. They encourage us when we need a boost of confidence. They celebrate with us when we accomplish our goals. They offer words of wisdom when we need advice. And, maybe most important, friends make life's journey a whole lot happier.

I can't imagine life without Raegan, Angie, Susan, Barb, Gena, Camille, Karen, Steph, Sylvia, Jenny, and the other important gal pals in my life. They are the thread of joy that runs through my life. From conversations about who is the best singer on *American Idol* to yummy pancake breakfasts at Cracker Barrel to all-day shopping trips to aerobic workouts on Saturday mornings—the times I spend with my best buddies bring me much joy.

Do you have special friends in your life? If so, how long has it been since you have taken time to get together with them, phone them, or drop them a card to say hello? Friendships take work. They require a time investment on your part. But they are definitely worth the time and effort.

If you don't have any close friends with whom you can share your life, ask God to send you some of those precious people. Or if you have been neglecting your friends, determine today to rekindle those relationships.

God didn't intend for us to go through life alone. He knew we would need each other. He knew that friends would add a dimension of happiness to our lives that we wouldn't be able to get anywhere else. So celebrate your friends today—and enjoy the journey of life a little bit more.

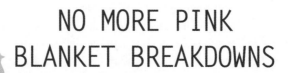

NO MORE PINK
BLANKET BREAKDOWNS

*Fixing our eyes on Jesus,
the pioneer and perfecter of faith.
For the joy set before him
he endured the cross.*
HEBREWS 12:2

"No!" Allyson, my then two-year-old, screamed at her older sister, Abby.

"That's mine!" she continued, jerking her white, silky blanket out of Abby's grip.

Abby immediately burst into tears, dropping to the floor in complete desperation. Then the real show began. She rolled from one side of the hallway to the other, screaming and breathing irregularly with each roll. She had lost her pink blanket, and now Allyson had reclaimed her white one. In her three-year-old reasoning, Abby believed that her happy life was over.

You might say she overreacted a bit.

I stepped over the traumatized toddler in an effort to find her beloved blanket. After checking all the usual spots, I noticed a ragged pink corner sticking out beneath a pile of stuffed animals in Abby's room. After a quick tug on the exposed material, the blanket mystery was solved.

Abby looked up through teary eyes and gazed at her long lost friend.

"My blankie!" she shrieked. With that, she jumped up, grabbed the blanket, and took her place next to Allyson, who was already watching Barney and Baby Bop on television.

The blanket was back and all was well in the world.

I've had many "pink blanket crises" in my life. Some rather insignificant thing goes wrong, and suddenly my world is destroyed. I cry and mope and pout—even have a few temper tantrums—and then God reveals the very simple solution I would have seen earlier had I not overreacted so badly.

If Abby had looked a little harder, she would have seen the telltale ragged pink corner of her blanket. But with impatience and desperation, she settled for her sister's white blanket—which was much easier to find because it was in the middle of the floor.

How many times have we settled for "Plan B" in our lives because we were too impatient and desperate to wait for God's perfect plan for us? How many times have we let the pink blanket crises in our lives overwhelm us, throw us into a blue funk, and steal our happiness?

It doesn't have to be that way. If we will keep our eyes fixed on Jesus, He will make sure we find our "pink blankets" every time—in His time.

WORMS AND ALL

Not that I have already obtained all this, or have already arrived at my goal, but I press on to take hold of that for which Christ Jesus took hold of me.
<small>PHILIPPIANS 3:12</small>

Do you ever feel overwhelmed, as if you are about to be buried in the pile of mounting laundry in your hamper? Have you ever felt like everyone at work thinks you're a moron in a nice suit? Do you ever feel like twenty-four hours is simply not enough time to accomplish everything on your to-do list?

There are times when I feel so overwhelmed and ill-equipped that I just want to run and hide under the bed. Then I think, *But God is God. He knew all of my shortcomings and faults before He entrusted me with all of these responsibilities, so He must see potential in me that I don't.*

Aren't you thankful that God looks at us through eyes of love instead of condemnation? On the days when I lose my temper with my family or fail to meet a work deadline or miss an opportunity to witness for Him simply because I'm too exhausted from the day-to-day burdens, I am immensely thankful that God is a patient, loving, always-seeing-the-best-in-me kind of God.

I am not a perfect mother. I mess up at work sometimes. And I often bite off more than I can chew. But God is changing me and perfecting me from glory to glory. And He is doing the same for you! He understands when we miss the mark. He cheers us on when we take a step closer to Him. He actually loves us even when we are at our very worst.

Think about that for a moment. God loves us so much that He gave His only Son for us—in spite of our shortcomings and less-than-perfect moments.

So the next time you feel overwhelmed, less than worthy, and totally clueless—ask God to help you see yourself the way He sees you. He adores you. You're the apple of His eye—even if you are a bit wormy at times. Now that's something to be happy about!

IT'S NOT ABOUT YOU

*"Lord Almighty, if you will
only look on your servant's
misery and remember me,
and not forget your servant but
give her a son, then I will give
him to the Lord for all the
days of his life."*
1 Samuel 1:11

There's a praise song called "It's All about You." Its words are simple but very powerful. The song goes, "It's all about You. It's all about You. It's all about You, Jesus."

In this "me, me, me" society, we forget that it's not all about us. It's all about the Lord. If we can keep our focus on Him and His will for our lives, we will be much happier people.

Hannah of the Bible struggled with the "me, me, me" mentality, too. She desperately wanted a son. Her husband's other wife had already given birth to several children, but Hannah was barren. Back then, when women couldn't get pregnant, society assumed they were cursed by God. Hannah wanted to give her husband a child. She no longer wanted to be the wife who couldn't get pregnant. She was tired of her rival mocking and harassing her because she had never given birth. You might say Hannah was consumed with her desperate situation. She was "me" focused.

Year after year Hannah believed God for a child. She cried out to God, begging for a son. But it wasn't until Hannah prayed a God-centered prayer—"LORD Almighty, if you will only look on your servant's misery and remember me, and not forget your servant but give her a son, then I will give him to the LORD for all the days of his life"—that she found happiness.

Once Hannah got her eyes off herself and on the

Lord, her prayer was answered. God gave her a son, Samuel, who played a very important role in history. (Read the book of 1 Samuel to learn more!) Then God gave Hannah several other children, too. See, you can never out-give God. He will always one-up you.

So if you're singing "me, me, me" instead of "It's all about You, Jesus," change your tune today. Take it from Hannah: The sooner you become more God-focused, the sooner you will find happiness.

SPEAK UP!

*We demolish arguments and every
pretension that sets itself up against
the knowledge of God, and we take
captive every thought to make it
obedient to Christ.*
2 CORINTHIANS 10:5

Joyce Meyer is one of my favorite Bible teachers, and she has written a wonderful book called *Battlefield of the Mind*. Truly, the mind is a battlefield. It's the place where faith and fear duke it out on a regular basis. It's the place where the devil can have a field day if you let him—so don't!

The minute a negative thought enters your mind, you need to cast it out. Now, maybe you're saying, "Michelle, I can't help myself. Bad thoughts come to my mind, and I can't seem to shake them." I can help you.

Do this for me: Try thinking a negative thought and saying, "Hallelujah, praise the Lord," at the same time. You can't do it, can you? The moment you speak, your mind has to think about what you're saying. Therefore you are no longer able to dwell on that negative thought.

You can use that knowledge to your advantage. The next time the devil plants a negative thought in your head, you can speak to that lie. If your mind is thinking, *You're never going to be able to pay your bills—you are always going to be poor,* say out loud, "According to the Word of God, my Lord supplies all of my needs. He owns the cattle on a thousand hills, and He will provide for me. I am blessed going in and blessed going out." As soon as you open your mouth to speak God's truth, your mind shifts gears from fear to faith.

Think about it. That's how Jesus fought the devil. When Satan came to Him with temptation, Jesus spoke to him saying, "It is written. . . ." Jesus didn't just *think* what the Scriptures said; He *spoke* those truths out loud. And the devil had to flee.

The next time you have a thought that is contrary to the Word of God, put the devil on the run! Speak what the Word says about that thought, and keep speaking those scriptures until you have crossed over from fear to faith. Pretty soon you will be winning the war in your mind on a regular basis. Guess what else you win? Peace and happiness.

DRIVE YOUR WAY
TO HAPPINESS

*Jesus answered, "It is written:
'Man shall not live on bread alone,
but on every word that comes from
the mouth of God.'"*
MATTHEW 4:4

Today's pace is insanely fast, isn't it? We go, go, go all the time. We drive to and from work; to and from school; to and from the health club; to and from soccer practice, gymnastics class, dance class, (fill in the blank) class; to and from dental and doctor appointments; to and from the grocery store, dry cleaner, and other places of business; to and from our children's games and events; and on and on it continues.

Sometimes I feel like I spend more time in my SUV than I do at home. Actually, if I added up the minutes, I probably do spend more time behind the wheel than at home. From where I live in Fort Worth, everything is about twenty-five minutes away, so I'm forced to drive a large percentage of every single day.

I used to sit in traffic and stress over things in my life. I'd drive like a maniac, trying to make my next appointment on time and occasionally bordering on road rage. I discovered that all that driving was literally driving me crazy, so I decided to make better use of the time.

Much to my tween-age daughters' disdain, I began turning off the car radio and tuning in to God. Sometimes I play praise and worship CDs. At other times I listen to teachings from my favorite preachers. Some days I listen to the Bible on CD. On still other days I use those minutes to commune with the Master. I pray out loud for everyone on my prayer list and spend time praising the Lord for everything good in my life.

Now, when I arrive at my destination, I'm not a stressed-out mess. Instead, I'm refueled with the love of God, fresh insights into His Word, and a renewed sense of happiness. I always joke that I have the most sanctified SUV in all of Texas. How sanctified is your vehicle?

Some people call it "multitasking" when you accomplish more than one thing at a time. I just call it "keeping my sanity in the midst of a crazy, stressed-out life." Don't dread your drive time anymore. Instead, use that time to draw closer to God.

Happy trails!

VARIETY IS THE SPICE OF LIFE

*"See, I am doing a new thing!
Now it springs up; do you not
perceive it? I am making a way
in the wilderness and streams
in the wasteland."*
Isaiah 43:19

An old proverb says, "Variety is the spice of life." It means that changes and new experiences make life delightful.

I can attest that that little proverb is packed full of truth. Last year I went on a fad diet that promised quick results. Okay, I know those quick fixes never work, but I was willing to try because a friend had raved about the results. So I called my friend and asked what groceries I needed to buy to start the diet the next morning.

"Pineapple. Lots and lots of pineapple. And tuna. Lots and lots of tuna."

"That's it?" I asked. "Pineapple and tuna?"

"That's it," my friend assured me.

So that's what I bought, and that's what I ate for seven days. Pineapple for breakfast, lunch, and supper on day one, and tuna for all three meals the next day. Then I repeated the cycle.

By the end of the week, my mouth was raw from pineapple acid, and I became nauseous just thinking about tuna. By the beginning of day eight, I vowed never to eat pineapple or tuna again. I had lost a couple of pounds, but I'd lost a few friends, too. It seems I was a bit "testy" on this diet. Actually, I was downright mean and had offended pretty much everyone around me during that week of fruit and fish.

When I began eating a variety of foods, I quickly

gained back those two pounds—and eventually my friends, too. But you know what else I got back? My joy.

I am convinced that we need variety in life to be happy.

God likes variety. Just look at the world around you for proof of that. God created an abundant variety of animals and plants—all for us to enjoy. He must have known we would get easily bored. So if you are stuck in the daily grind of life, never exploring new parts of the world, never meeting new people, never trying new things, spice it up! Oh, and a word of advice: Avoid tuna for breakfast at all costs.

GET AN ATTITUDE ADJUSTMENT

And as the Spirit of the Lord works within us, we become more and more like him and reflect his glory even more.
2 Corinthians 3:18 NLT

Have you ever been to a chiropractor? Many people today are turning to chiropractors for relief from pain and even for preventive health care. I used to be a skeptic until I actually went to a chiropractor. Wow! I had no idea the difference a little adjustment could make in my life.

With just one or two small adjustments—a crack here, a pop there—my chiropractor put my hips back in alignment. Immediately, I felt better. After just a few treatments, the before and after X-rays proved what I already knew. I was better—a lot better.

It's the same way with God. He can make just one or two small adjustments to your heart, and you will have a lot better attitude. With an adjustment here (getting rid of jealousy) and a tweak there (taking care of that anger), God can totally rework your heart. He will fix things you didn't even know needed fixing—and before you know it, your joy will return. You'll feel better than you have felt in years.

Of course, once you are back in alignment, you will need to go to God for maintenance work—just as I have to return to the chiropractor periodically to keep myself in alignment. God will constantly work on your heart to keep it in line with His Word and His plan for your life. That's how we maintain good spiritual health.

So how is your heart today? Are you out of whack

and in need of an adjustment? If so, turn to the Great Physician. If you are struggling with worry, anger, unforgiveness, or anything else that isn't right, ask God to "give you an adjustment." He will! He wants to see you walking in perfect spiritual health.

Go ahead. Get an attitude adjustment today!

PERFECTION IS
A MOVING TARGET

To all perfection I see a limit;
but your commands are boundless.
PSALM 119:96

"Congratulations on a great presentation," says a co-worker. "You did a good job!"

"Yeah, but not good enough," you mumble. "I totally messed up that last point."

Does this conversation sound familiar? If so, you are probably a perfectionist. (Or, in my case, a recovering perfectionist.)

Geoffrey F. Fisher said, "When you aim for perfection, you discover it's a moving target." True perfectionists know the validity of that statement.

Do you know the problem with trying to be perfect? You always end up disappointed in yourself and others, because no matter how hard you try, you'll never be perfect.

That's not a negative confession, it's just reality—which is why being a perfectionist is so frustrating. Once you understand that perfection is only a goal—not a requirement—you will be a lot happier in all that you do.

Go ahead and shoot for perfection, but don't beat yourself up when you miss impossible goals. Be sure to celebrate the goals you do reach.

Maybe you haven't achieved the weight you put on your driver's license (as if any of us has!), but you did lose five pounds this month. Don't dwell on the fact that you didn't meet that ideal weight. Instead, celebrate your five-pound weight loss. Maybe you didn't sell the most real estate in your office this month, but you did achieve a personal best. Celebrate your accomplishment!

God wants you to celebrate you and the good things you achieve. He doesn't expect you to be perfect all the time, so why should you expect that? God knows you're human; after all, He made you!

Ask God to help you feel happier with yourself and your accomplishments. Start celebrating the person that God made you to be. And always remember this: You may never be perfect, but you are perfectly loved by God. Now that's something to be happy about!

PRAY YOUR WAY TO HAPPINESS

"But to you who are listening I say: Love your enemies, do good to those who hate you, bless those who curse you, pray for those who mistreat you."
LUKE 6:27–28

"That sweater looks great on you," your catty cousin says. "I wish I could wear bold pieces like you, but I'm just too petite. You carry it off well, though, since you're much bigger."

Ouch.

You've just been given a left-handed compliment, and you didn't even see it coming. Your cousin continues on her path of ugliness.

"I like your new hairstyle, too," she adds. "It takes the focus off your nose, which has never been one of your best features."

Okay, the "old you" wants to deck her and repent later, right?

But God wants you to pray for her.

Say what?

I know, I know. It seems totally unnatural and flat-out wrong to pray for someone who has hurt your feelings. It seems crazy to pray for that person who loves being ugly to you. But it is what Jesus says to do in His Word. He doesn't say you have to like it, but He does say you have to do it.

Know why? Because God knows that unforgiveness, bitterness, and anger will destroy us if we let those emotions fester inside. He tells us to pray for our enemies because it is impossible to be mad at someone and pray for that person at the same time. (Believe me—I've tried it.)

Honestly, you're going to need God's intervention when you first embark on praying for your enemies. That's okay, because God will help you. Just ask Him.

The next time one of your gal pals acts ugly toward you, don't fight back. Instead, pray for her. Pray for your enemies by faith even if you do it with a red face and through gritted teeth. If you will do your part, God will do His.

He may not change your enemy's actions, but He will change the way you feel about that person. Then, the next time you see her or him, you will have happiness and love in your heart instead of malice and anger. Determine today to pray—especially for your enemies!

SAY NO TO STRIFE

Do not repay anyone evil for evil.
Be careful to do what is right in
the eyes of everyone.
ROMANS 12:17

Sometimes you just have to fight the urge to fight.

You will have opportunities every day to engage in a battle of words, but you need to resist that urge.

Even if your daughter breaks curfew and lies about it. Even if your spouse spends a lot of money without discussing it with you. Even if your coworker takes credit for a project you orchestrated. No matter what, you need to resist the urge to fight.

Nothing can suck the joy out of life faster than strife.

Proverbs 17:1 (CEV) says, "A dry crust of bread eaten in peace and quiet is better than a feast eaten where everyone argues." In other words, no matter how lavish your surroundings or how healthy your bank account, you will never be happy if you let strife exist in your home or workplace.

If you have strife in your life, get it out of there today! James 3:16 says that where strife is, every evil work is also lurking. Constant strife is an invitation for Satan to enter your home. It's like saying, "Come on in, Mr. Devil, and make yourself comfortable. Oh, and invite all of your evil friends, too—jealousy, fear, bitterness, hate, depression, and unforgiveness."

That's why strife is so dangerous.

Proverbs 20:3 (NIV) says, "It is to one's honor to avoid strife, but every fool is quick to quarrel." Don't be a fool. No matter how badly you want to retaliate, don't give in. It's not worth it. Fight the urge to fight!

When you feel yourself getting angry, ask God to help you control your temper. Instead of yelling at your daughter or your spouse or your co-worker, stop and praise God for them. Then pray for them. Praise and prayer will drive strife right out of your life, making room for more happiness.

SOAK IN THE WORD

Oh, how I love your law!
I meditate on it all day long.
PSALM 119:97

After a long, hard day, don't you just love to soak in a bathtub full of bubbles? Your mind is tired. Your feet are sore. Your head is throbbing. So you escape into a hot, soothing, bubbly bath.

That's one of my favorite things to do. If I could, I would soak in the tub so long that my entire body would become "pruney." There's just nothing like a bubble bath—it's my happy place. A sense of peace and rest and happiness washes over me as I soak.

Know what else brings peace and rest? Soaking in God's Word. I'm talking about reading the Word in such a way that you are totally immersed in it. When you spend time in the scripture, it becomes alive in you. It changes you from the inside out. God's Word replaces stress with peace, sickness with healing, anger with compassion, hate with love, worry with faith, weariness with energy, and sadness with happiness.

If you don't know where to begin soaking, start with Psalm 119:10–16, which is all about loving and honoring the Word of God. It says:

> *I seek you with all my heart;*
>   *do not let me stray from your commands.*
> *I have hidden your word in my heart*
>   *that I might not sin against you.*
> *Praise be to you, LORD;*
>   *teach me your decrees.*

With my lips I recount
  all the laws that come from your mouth.
I rejoice in following your statutes
  as one rejoices in great riches.
I meditate on your precepts
  and consider your ways.
I delight in your decrees;
  I will not neglect your word.

Soaking every day in God's Word will keep you balanced, renewed, and ready to tackle whatever comes your way. You will begin to bubble over with joy and become a better person in every way. And you won't even get "pruney" in the process. So go ahead. Soak it up!

BE HAPPY WHILE YOU WAIT

He told them, "You don't get to know the time. Timing is the Father's business."
ACTS 1:7 MSG

Patience.

Just saying the word is painful, isn't it?

Waiting is never fun and is often challenging, but it is also a part of life. Often it is part of God's ultimate plan. The problem is that we don't wait very well. We are an impatient people. Think back to Sarah in the Bible. She had a patience problem, didn't she?

God promised that Sarah and Abraham would have a son, but years passed and she didn't become pregnant. Sarah was feeling the pressure. She knew Abraham was supposed to be the father of many nations, yet she couldn't bear him even one child. Don't you imagine she was thinking, *Okay, God. Where are You in all of this?*

Sarah became impatient. She got tired of waiting on God's plan and eventually came up with her own plan. She decided to move things along a bit and help God out. (Ever been there? Me, too.) So Sarah told Abraham she wanted him to lay with her Egyptian maid, Hagar, in order to produce a child. Abraham listened to his wife, did as she requested, and Hagar became pregnant with Ishmael.

But Ishmael was not the child of promise. The whole situation Sarah created became the source of much aggravation—and even more delay in Sarah's life. In fact, Ishmael was fourteen years old before Isaac, the child of promise, was born. Sarah finally gave birth to the son God had promised her, but it was in God's time—not hers.

The Ishmaels in life never bring us happiness. They are always the source of frustration. We end up birthing Ishmaels and then asking God to bless the plan we formulated because we were too impatient to wait on God's perfect plan.

Let's learn from Sarah's story. Let's endeavor to wait on God and His perfect plan. And let's wait in joy and expectancy, praising God for what is to come. His plan—His promise—is always worth the wait!

BITE YOUR TONGUE

"Do you really love life?
Do you want to be happy?
Then stop saying cruel things
and quit telling lies."
1 PETER 3:10 CEV

The tongue is one of the smallest parts of our body, but it packs a lot of power.

The Bible speaks to that truth in James 3:2–6 (CEV):

> *All of us do many wrong things. But if you can control your tongue, you are mature and able to control your whole body.*
>
> *By putting a bit into the mouth of a horse, we can turn the horse in different directions. It takes strong winds to move a large sailing ship, but the captain uses only a small rudder to make it go in any direction. Our tongues are small too, and yet they brag about big things.*
>
> *It takes only a spark to start a forest fire! The tongue is like a spark. It is an evil power that dirties the rest of the body and sets a person's entire life on fire with flames that come from hell itself.*

Well, that pretty much says it all. We have to control our tongues if we want to live a happy life, but we can't do it alone. We have to ask for God's help because we can't tame our own tongues.

Here's the good news: At the very moment you became a Christian, you were infused with power from heaven. You have the Holy Spirit living inside you, helping you and guiding you. You have the fruit of the Spirit operating in your life, and one of those fruits is self-control. Ask God to help you grow in this area so that you can control that tongue of yours. He will do it.

Pray this out loud with me right now:

> *Father, I thank You for self-control. I thank You that my tongue only speaks words in agreement with Your Word and nothing else. Holy Spirit, keep a watch over my mouth so that I only speak words that bring glory to the Father. In Jesus' name, amen.*

Now, go out and speak good things—good things about yourself, your situation, your future, your family, and the Lord. When you feel tempted to say negative things that are in direct conflict with the Word of God, zip it up. Your verse for that moment is, "Be still and know that I am God." Keep control of your mouth, and you will enjoy a much happier life.

DON'T LET YOUR KIDS
GET YOU DOWN

"There's hope for your children."
JEREMIAH 31:17 MSG

If you are a parent, you will be a parent until the day you go to heaven. No matter how old your children are today, they are still your babies. You love them. You want the best for them. You'd give your life for them.

That is why it hurts our hearts so much when they are away from God, rebelling against our heavenly Father. If your kids are away from God right now, happiness may seem impossible. But remember, all things are possible with God.

You can be happy even if your kids are away from God. But, you say, "Michelle, how can I be happy when my children's lives are such a mess? You don't know how badly they've messed up."

No, I don't know. But God does, and what's more, He cares about your children even more than you do. How can you be happy in the midst of heartache and turmoil? You can be happy because, though the battle isn't over, we know how it ends. We win!

The devil cannot have your kids. Those children are your seed! I don't care how bad it looks today. I don't care if your son is in prison or your daughter is suicidal—God is well able to turn those situations around.

Your job in all of this? Pray for your children and stay positive, because the joy of the Lord is your strength.

If you don't have kids of your own, pray for your nieces and nephews or the other children in your life. But don't pray faithless, whiney prayers. Pray power-packed, Word-based prayers, such as:

> *Father, I thank You that my children are Your workmanship, created for good works that You have prepared for them [see Ephesians 2:10]. I thank You that they will return to You and fulfill the good plan that You have for them [see Jeremiah 29:11]. I praise You, Lord, that my children are taught by You and that they will have great peace [see Isaiah 54:13]. Amen.*

If you keep praying those Word-based prayers and praising the Lord for the breakthrough in your kids' lives, you can have joy in the midst of turmoil. Start today and enjoy life. Your children are blessed of the Lord!

THERE'S HAPPINESS
IN WISDOM

Get wisdom, get understanding;
do not forget my words
or turn away from them.
PROVERBS 4:5

As I sat among the other writers, I listened intently as one author insisted that an agent is required for success in the publishing world. Her arguments were strong and convincing. I had pretty much decided to contact an agent who had shown an interest in my writing when another writer stood and shared his horror stories about past agents. "By the time you can get an agent," he said, "you don't really need one."

By the end of that session, I was so confused that I wanted to run out of the room screaming. Instead, I retreated to my room and sought God for an answer. I prayed for direction and began reading God's Word. Turning to the book of Joshua, my eyes fell on a verse that says, "Haven't I commanded you? Strength! Courage! Don't be timid; don't get discouraged. GOD, your God, is with you every step you take" (Joshua 1:9 THE MESSAGE).

The phrase "God is with you every step you take" went off in my spirit. It was as if God was telling me, "Hey, I am right here with you on this publishing journey. Don't sweat it. Just enjoy it." I meditated on that verse for quite a while, then heard that still, small voice say, *I'll be your agent.* That was the wisdom I needed. It settled the matter—once and for all—in my mind and heart.

I have a lot of Christian writer friends who use agents and love them. I'm not "anti-agent" at all. But

God had given me clear direction that afternoon, and His direction was not to enter into a contractual agreement with an agent. I no longer had to wonder if I needed an agent. After all, I had the best agent in the world!

I am so thankful that I can go to God for wisdom in any situation—big or small. I can search His Word and find the exact answer I need at the exact time I need it. He is the ultimate expert. He doesn't have to consult with anyone to give you an answer—He *is* the answer!

No matter what you need today, you can go to God for His counsel. He will give you the wisdom you desire and settle the question for you once and for all. There is such peace in that reality and, oh, such joy!

CONTENTMENT—YEAH, IT'S POSSIBLE!

*Be content with such
things as you have.*
HEBREWS 13:5 NKJV

I once read a cartoon that said, "The grass may look greener on the other side, but it still has to be mowed."

That's so true, isn't it?

Envy leads to discontentment leads to depression leads to you-don't-want-to-get-out-of-bed-in-the-morning. The devil loves to show you how miserable your life is, then shift your focus to how wonderful your friend's life is. He will say things like, "Your husband doesn't like to spend time with you. He is always too busy for you. But Sue's husband can't wait to take her out. He adores spending quality time with her."

If you meditate on the devil's line of thinking long enough, you will fall into envious sin. And if you are not quick to repent, you will find yourself vulnerable to the possibility of infidelity. That's how the devil works, leading you into sin little by little.

We have all heard that the devil is the father of lies—but he's also the master of illusion. He will show you someone else's life and lead you to believe that hers is perfect, while yours is far from it. Suddenly, you will forget about all the good things worth celebrating in your life and focus on the bad stuff. Before long you will be discontent and void of any joy in your life.

Do you know what combats discontentment? Praise.

The next time the devil comes to you with "the grass is greener in your neighbor's yard" line of thinking, stop and praise the Lord. Say, "Lord, I praise You for my spouse—for his hard work and strength and [insert an appropriate positive here]. I ask that You will give us the time we need together, and I thank You that we have a wonderful life ahead of us."

It may be that your spouse doesn't spend quality time with you right now, but that's not the end of the story. Don't spend your time thinking discontented thoughts. Instead, spend your time speaking the Word of God and knocking on your heavenly Father's door until you get the desired result. The Word says God "calls into being things that were not" (Romans 4:17).

So call it forth! Praise the Lord for the happiness in your life and the happy things to come.

LET GO AND LET GOD

Instead of shame and dishonor, you will inherit a double portion of prosperity and everlasting joy. "For I, the LORD, love justice. I hate robbery and wrongdoing. I will faithfully reward my people for their suffering and make an everlasting covenant with them."

ISAIAH 61:7–8 NLT

Did you know that God is a God of payback? It's true. You can totally trust Him to bring about justice. I've experienced that truth in my own life.

A few years ago I worked with an editor who treated me so poorly that I actually questioned my calling to write. At that point in my career, I'd already written nineteen books, but she made me question every piece I'd ever written.

She became so ugly toward me—impossible to work with, actually—that I eventually paid back my advance and withdrew my book from that publishing house. I had never done that before and have never done it since. I was heartbroken. I felt like a failure. I wondered where God was in that whole situation.

I'll be honest—I was mad. I wasn't feeling love for her. Every time I heard her name mentioned, I'd feel ickiness flooding my heart. I knew I had to give that hurt to God and move on, but it was difficult. Finally, I came clean with God and asked Him to heal my hurting heart—and I prayed for that editor who had hurt me so deeply.

I didn't feel an immediate change toward that editor, but by faith I kept on praying for her. Eventually, that ickiness left and God restored my heart.

Not only did God restore my heart, but also He restored my career. And when God restores something, He always makes it better than it was before. That one-book contract that I lost turned into a four-book contract with a different publisher. And the editor at the new publishing house has become one of my dearest friends.

God had a plan all along, but had I stayed mad and let bitterness overtake my heart, I would have tied God's hands. I truly believe my writing career would have ended.

Sometimes you just have to "let go and let God." He wants to be your vindicator. He wants to restore the things you have lost in your life, but you have to let Him. Trade in your hurt for happiness today, and watch God work.

OFFENSE IS A
BLESSING BLOCKER

[Love] is not self-seeking.
1 Corinthians 13:5

Are you easily offended? If so, your joy level is probably nonexistent. How do I know? Because if you are offended all the time, you will never walk in the blessings God has for you.

Offense puts a roadblock on your path to blessing. Think of offense as a "blessing blocker," because that is what it really is.

You will have opportunities for taking offense every day, so you have to choose to walk in love. At times, doing so is harder than at other times, but you must turn away from offense and turn toward God. If you don't, you might just miss something wonderful.

Take Jairus, the synagogue ruler, for example. He came to Jesus because his little girl was dying. Having heard that Jesus was able to heal the sick, Jairus didn't send one of the men who worked for him to call the Lord, but instead went himself.

You know the story. He finds Jesus and asks Him to come home with him to heal his daughter, and Jesus agrees. Then suddenly, the woman with an issue of blood touches the hem of Jesus' garment and is completely healed. Jesus stops to find out who touched Him, and during His interaction with the woman, Jairus learns that his daughter has just passed away.

At that moment, Jairus had an opportunity to be offended. He could have been really angry with the woman for holding up the Master—the One who was to heal his little girl. Jairus could have been angry with Jesus and said, "If You wouldn't have taken so long with her, my little girl would still be alive!" But Jairus didn't choose offense. He simply stood his ground of faith. The end result? Jesus healed Jairus's little girl.

What offense are you holding in your heart today? More important, what blessings are you missing because of that offense? Don't block your blessings any longer. No offense is worth that. Repent and ask God to help you get over any past offenses and steer clear of any future ones.

Now, get back on the path that leads to your blessings and happiness. The road looks clear from here!

GET A POSITIVE PERSPECTIVE

*Now faith is confidence in
what we hope for and assurance
about what we do not see.*
HEBREWS 11:1

Toby Slough, senior pastor of Cross Timbers Community Church in Argyle, Texas, says, "Never underestimate the power of perspective."

Having a positive perspective is vital. It can change the whole atmosphere in which you move.

Do you remember the story of the prophet Elisha and his servant in 2 Kings 6? The king of Aram was angry with Elisha because Elisha was always spoiling his plans to destroy Israel. Every time the king and his troops would plan an attack against the Israelites, Elisha would warn Israel's king. Finally, the king of Aram could stand it no longer, so he sent his army to capture Elisha.

That night Aram's army surrounded the city where Elisha and his servant were sleeping. When they awoke the next morning, the situation appeared grim. Elisha's servant panicked, saying, "Oh no, my lord! What shall we do?" (verse 15). Elisha didn't panic. Instead, he prayed, "Open his eyes, LORD, so that he may see" (verse 17). And God did, so the servant could see the hills full of horses and chariots of fire, totally surrounding and protecting him and Elisha. Suddenly, the king of Aram's army didn't seem quite so threatening.

The servant certainly got a new perspective, didn't he? He went from total panic mode to "Bring it on!" Once he saw that God "had their back," he was no longer fearful. You might say he got a positive perspective.

That's what we all need today—a healthy positive perspective. Why not ask God to help you see every situation through His eyes? Ask Him to help you see your world differently so that you can face every challenge with a positive attitude. If you will face life in faith, not fear, you will enjoy every day—no matter what life may bring.

FEELING KIND OF GROUCHY?

*And you will always give
thanks for everything
to God the Father in the name
of our Lord Jesus Christ.*
EPHESIANS 5:20 NLT

Remember Oscar the Grouch on *Sesame Street?* He and all of his buddies are back in fashion now. You see them on fashion-forward folks everywhere. My tween-age daughters love to wear *Sesame Street* characters on their T-shirts—especially Oscar and Elmo.

One such Oscar T-shirt says: "Warning: Feeling Kind of Grouchy Today." Now, be honest—is your usual mood worthy of donning an Oscar the Grouch T-shirt?

If you're grouchy more often than you're happy, you need to ask God to turn your attitude around. Ask Him to help you quit complaining, and start praising instead. Complaining and grouching your way through life is no way to live. It sabotages your future, and it angers God. The Israelites found that out the hard way. Consequently, their journey to the Promised Land took them forty years instead of the forty days it should have taken.

Remember the story? God had just rescued the people from slavery in Egypt. He had even caused the Red Sea to part so they could walk across on dry land. But still they complained. In no time at all, the Israelites tired of God's miracle manna, grouching that they preferred the leeks and cucumbers of Egypt. Because of their ungrateful and complaining attitudes, they were forced to wander around in the wilderness for many years.

If you have been wandering in your own wilderness lately, maybe it's because your attitude is ungrateful and grouchy. God can't work in your life to the extent He would like if you are grouching around all the time. If that's your attitude, change today. Ask God to fill you with His joy. Start each day by praising God instead of murmuring your way through breakfast. Put that Oscar the Grouch attitude where it belongs—in the trash can.

GET A JOY INFUSION

*"Do not sorrow, for the joy
of the Lord is your strength."*
NEHEMIAH 8:10 NKJV

The Word tells us that the devil comes to steal and destroy (John 10:10)—and one of the things he loves to take from Christians is their joy. Do you know why? Because the joy of the Lord is our strength, and the devil knows that truth. He will do everything he can to take that strength from us.

That is why you have to be aware of the devil's crafty schemes for stealing your joy. For instance, if going to the congested grocery store on Saturday afternoon steals your joy, go shopping on a weekday evening or ask your spouse to make the Saturday run. If driving in rush-hour traffic stresses you out and steals your joy, try avoiding the crush by working out after quitting time and driving home later when the traffic has thinned. Or if you must drive at that crazy time of day, listen to praise and worship music while sitting in traffic.

You can do other things to help keep your joy at an optimum level, as well. Make sure you get enough sleep each night. Exercise on a regular basis. Eat a nutritionally balanced diet. Drink plenty of water. Don't overload your schedule with too many activities, which can lead to stress. Surround yourself with positive people. Finally, make time to laugh each day.

Ask God to give you a daily infusion of joy. Keep your heart and head full of the Word of God. Meditate on scriptures that deal with joy, such as:

- "Fill my heart with joy when their grain and new wine abound" (Psalm 4:7).
- "You make known to me the path of life; you will fill me with joy in your presence, with eternal pleasures at your right hand" (Psalm 16:11).
- "Restore to me the joy of your salvation and grant me a willing spirit, to sustain me" (Psalm 51:12).

God has an endless supply of joy awaiting you, and the devil can't steal it unless you let him. So keep hold of your joy—and refill your supply often.

BE A RISK TAKER

"Come on!" Jesus said.
Peter then got out of the boat and started
walking on the water toward him.
MATTHEW 14:29 CEV

When you think of the apostle Peter, what comes to mind first? If you are like most people, you remember him for denying Jesus three times the night of the Lord's arrest. But Peter is also remembered for trying to walk on the water. Though he failed Jesus at a crucial moment, he had often been the most vocal and ambitious of the disciples. He was a risk taker.

When all the other disciples saw Jesus walking on the waves toward their boat, they chose to stay in the safety of their vessel. Peter was the only one with faith enough to take that first step outside the boat. He never considered his own welfare, even though the wind was stiff and the water turbulent. He only knew that Jesus was out there, welcoming him to come.

Live your life as a risk taker for Jesus. It will never be boring. You will discover that there is great happiness in serving Him in such an all-out way.

As Christians, we need to be willing to do what God asks us to do—no matter what. So if He says, "Teach the seventh grade girls' Sunday school class," you should be willing to do just that—no matter how unqualified you may feel. If God urges you to invite the most aloof woman in your neighborhood to attend church, you should be willing to "step outside the boat" and ask her.

When Peter's faith weakened and he began to

sink, Jesus was there to rescue him. And Jesus will be there for you if you should run into trouble. Trust God and listen for His quiet urgings. Get out of the boat and make a difference today. You will be so happy you did!

WHAT A BARGAIN!

"For God so loved the world that he gave his one and only Son, that whoever believes in him shall not perish but have eternal life."
JOHN 3:16

There's something intoxicating about finding a great deal. Some call it thrilling. Some call it a shopping high. I call it pure happiness.

If you have never been to a yard sale, a consignment shop, or your town's Goodwill store, you are missing out. From designer scarves to eclectic furniture, you will find it all at these bargain meccas. What they say about bargain shopping is true: "One person's junk is another person's treasure."

I have found many treasures on bargain-hunting trips. Once I found a Louis Vuitton scarf for only ninety-nine cents. Another time, a Carole Little suit for three dollars. On another occasion, I came home with a Banana Republic leather jacket for only six dollars.

Those kinds of buys make you want to shout from the rooftop. But those bargains pale in comparison to the greatest bargain of all time—salvation.

God gave His only Son to die on the cross so that we could have eternal life. All we have to do is ask Him to forgive us of our sins and accept Him as our Lord and Savior. We receive eternal life, healing, peace, love, wisdom, prosperity, joy, and so much more—all free to us, since Jesus has paid the price for our sins! Now, that's a bargain really worth shouting from the rooftops!

Make sure you share the love of Jesus with all

those you encounter. Tell them about the treasure you have found in Jesus, and encourage them to pray this prayer with you:

> *Dear Father, we thank You for sending Jesus to die on the cross for us. We thank You for loving us that much. Today we ask Him to forgive us of all our sins, and we accept Him as our Lord and Savior. We love You. Amen.*

Sharing Jesus with the world around you will bring much happiness to you, and it will bring much happiness to those who accept Him as their Lord and Savior. Don't be afraid to witness for the Lord. He will open doors for you to share your faith. Just be obedient to walk through them.

SIMPLIFY YOUR LIFE

*A devout life does bring wealth,
but it's the rich simplicity of
being yourself before God.
Since we entered the world penniless
and will leave it penniless, if we
have bread on the table and shoes
on our feet, that's enough.*
1 TIMOTHY 6:6–8 MSG

Comedian, actor, and singer Eddie Cantor once said, "Slow down and enjoy life. It's not only the scenery you miss by going too fast—you also miss the sense of where you are going and why."

I have learned that those words are quite true.

When my daughter Abby was about five, she loved to draw and color. She would spend hours making pictures, which gave me time to write articles and finish assignments on my laptop. I was working full-time for a magazine and still trying to write my own books and do work for other publications during downtime. My motives were good. I wanted to work more, earn more money, and pay off the debt we had accumulated from our cross-country move and the purchase of our new home. However, I had become a workaholic without even realizing it—and I had lost my joy in the midst of it.

"Here, Mommy, I drew a picture for you," Abby beamed as she handed me her drawing.

As I looked at it, tears welled in my eyes. She had drawn a picture of me typing at my computer. She hadn't drawn a picture of me playing with her or her sister, Ally, like she had drawn for her daddy. Why? Because that's how Abby saw me—a mom behind a computer screen. My heart was broken. But God is merciful, and as I turned to Him for guidance and healing, He took care of both.

Today I still work full-time because I truly love what I do—but I also make my family a priority. I make sure that my husband and daughters know how important they are to me, and that I'm available to them even when I'm under the tightest of deadlines. We spend time jogging together, going to see movies, watching *American Idol*, playing with our dogs—whatever. We just have fun together.

I don't want to reach the end of my life only to realize I have worked away the years and neglected the people who are most important. I don't want you to make that mistake, either.

Are you a workaholic? Do you need to simplify your life by making changes that will allow you more downtime with your loved ones? We can't get back yesterday, but we can cherish today and all of our tomorrows. Simplify your life and watch your joy return.

GOD ISN'T
MAD AT YOU

*"I have loved you with
an everlasting love."*
JEREMIAH 31:3

Many people go through life with the idea that God is mad at them. Because of this errant thinking, they flee the Father instead of running into His loving arms. Maybe you are one of those people. Maybe you have worn out several pairs of track shoes running from God. Well, I want to revolutionize your thinking today.

God isn't mad at you!

Let that sink deep into your spirit for a moment. God isn't mad at you; in fact, He loves you! He has loved you since before you were even formed in your mother's womb. And His greatest desire is to be in a close relationship with you. He longs to spend time with you and share His love with you.

But maybe you're saying, "Michelle, I have been a no-good, dirty, rotten crudball my whole life. There is no way that God could love me."

Listen: God is in the business of loving crudballs, and He wants you to know that you don't have to be a crudball anymore. The Word says, "Anyone who belongs to Christ is a new person. The past is forgotten, and everything is new" (2 Corinthians 5:17 CEV). So if you have asked Jesus to cleanse your heart and become the Lord of your life, your crudball days are behind you. The Lord doesn't see you as a crudball. He sees you as His precious child, and He adores you.

Quit picturing God as a mean old guy in the sky,

holding a club in His hand, ready to bop you every time you make a mistake. That is not who God is. He isn't looking for perfect people, because He knows there aren't any. He is looking for people who will love and honor Him. Why? Because He wants to be your daddy. He wants to bless you. He wants to give you the kind of joy that comes only from heaven.

Quit running away from God, and start running to Him. Put away those track shoes and let the Father love on you today. That's where true happiness lies.

GOD IS AT WORK

I am trusting you, O Lord, saying,
*   "You are my God!"*
My future is in your hands.
Psalm 31:14–15 nlt

Did you know that God is often working most when we sense it the least?

As I reflect on my life, I can see that has often been the case. Those times when things looked the worst, when it seemed as if God had gone on vacation, were the times when God was working behind the scenes on my behalf.

We discover that our timing is not always God's timing. Actually, our timing is almost never God's timing. We want instant gratification in our give-it-to-me-now society. We want to pray and have God answer us by noon. But God usually doesn't work like that.

Take it from Noah.

He followed God's leading and built an ark—even though it had never rained before. He obeyed God's instructions perfectly. Pairs of all the animals began to fill the big boat, and finally, Noah and his family boarded the ark and waited for the rain.

You know the story. It rained forty days and forty nights, and Noah and his family were the only ones spared. The boat ride, however, was much longer than forty days. It went on for months and months! Think about that for a moment: Noah and his family are on an ark with a bunch of smelly animals for months on end, and there's no land in sight. Can't you just hear his wife saying, "Yeah, great plan, Noah. Where's the land? Did God tell you how long we'd have to float around with a bunch of stinking creatures?"

You can imagine Noah, every day looking out the ark's windows, only to see water on every side. Finally, Noah sends out a bird, hoping to get proof that land has appeared somewhere—but the bird comes back empty-beaked. It must have looked like God had forgotten them, that they were doomed to ride around on a big boat forever.

But God was at work, slowly diminishing the water every day—even those days when Noah saw water all around. In time the ark hit dry land, and Noah and his family left the ark to enjoy God's promise.

Are you on a long ark ride right now? If so, rejoice! Be happy today—even if you can't see anything changing. Land is near. God hasn't forgotten you. He is at work behind the scenes.

DON'T PUT IT OFF

Again He sets a definite day, [a new] Today, [and gives another opportunity of securing that rest,] saying through David after so long a time, in the words already quoted, Today, if you would hear His voice, and when you hear it, do not harden your hearts.

HEBREWS 4:7 AMP

Have you been procrastinating stopping procrastination? If you answered yes, it is time to stop procrastinating. Getting a handle on procrastination will help you become a more productive, successful, and happy person.

Why do we put tasks off to the last possible minute when doing so causes missed opportunities, frenzied work hours, stress, resentment, and guilt?

Some people procrastinate because it allows them to avoid doing something they feel forced to do. If that is your mind-set, outsmart yourself. Tell yourself, "I don't have to do this task. Sure, if I don't do it, there will be consequences, like missing a deadline and disappointing someone, but it's not a matter of life or death." That should replace the "have to" thinking with a "want to" mind-set. You will want to start the project so you won't miss that deadline or disappoint that person.

Here are some other ways to combat procrastination:

1. *Replace "finish it" with "begin it."* Do your task in small increments. Beginning the task is half the battle.
2. *Focus on the "now," not the future.* Don't borrow tomorrow's trouble today. Focus on the task at hand—not on next week's to-do list. Learn to take life hour by hour

so you don't feel overwhelmed.

3.   *Replace perfectionism with good work.* If
     you think you have to do everything
     perfectly, you might become too over-
     whelmed even to begin. Give yourself the
     luxury of being human.

You will discover that God will give you grace for
today—not yesterday or tomorrow. So focus on living
today for God and accomplishing the things you *must*
do today. That will take the pressure off, and you will
be able to enter His rest. Where there is rest, there
is happiness. So be happy today. Don't worry about
tomorrow, and don't delay your dreams with procrastination. Get going, now!

PENCIL IN PRAYER

*Very early in the morning,
while it was still dark, Jesus got up,
left the house and went off to a
solitary place, where he prayed.*
MARK 1:35

Are you a list maker? If you don't have a to-do list for the day, do you feel lost?

Me, too.

Many people find refuge in a to-do list, using it as a map for every twenty-four-hour period. If you are a true to-do lister, then you don't do anything that is not on the list, right? It goes against everything in you to divert from the master list. (I have your number, don't I?)

What does a to-do list have to do with prayer? Just this: If you really want to be serious about prayer, you are going to have to pencil it into your daily schedule. That will be a reminder that prayer is a priority in your life. And where prayer is a priority, happiness is a by-product.

You can pray all the time—continually—as 1 Thessalonians 5:17 says, but you can also set a designated time for really intense, focused prayer. Mark 1:35 tells us that Jesus chose to do His praying in the early morning, while it was still dark. But if you are not a morning person, pray in the afternoon or evening. Do whatever works for you—just do it.

If you have trouble staying awake during prayer time or keeping your "prayer appointment," why not get a prayer partner? Ask a friend or a family member to help. You can either meet together in person or pray over the telephone—whatever arrangement works best for your schedule. I have a wonderful prayer pal in Illinois named Sarah. She and I support each other, cry with each other, and pray for one another's needs. We may not pray together every day, but I know she is praying for me daily—and she knows that I am praying for her, too. That sort of prayer commitment with someone else will cause you to hit your knees on a more regular basis.

Now is the time to get serious about prayer. Pray for favor with your colleagues, friends, and family. Pray for wisdom as you make life-altering decisions. Pray for guidance as you follow your dreams. Pray for the men and women serving this country. Pray for the president and your state and local leaders. Pray protection and blessings over your family. Simply thank the Lord for His goodness and mercy. Just pray. Think of prayer as an investment in your ultimate happiness.

DO YOU SPEAK CHRISTIANESE?

"Let your light so shine before men, that they may see your good works and glorify your Father in heaven."
MATTHEW 5:16 NKJV

Ahh. . .the superspiritual. People of all stripes are turned off by them. That sickeningly sweet, superficial spirituality will never do God any good. In fact, it makes Him look bad. So if you are a superspiritual kind of Christian, break free from Christianese! Stop trying to be so spiritual and worrying about impressing others with your Christian ways. There is no peace and joy in that way of living. Instead, focus on your daily walk with God, and let your faith speak loudly all by itself.

Jesus was a carpenter—and the Son of God. He did good work for His earthly father and for His heavenly Father. People were drawn to Him everywhere He went. Successful Christians have learned to follow His example.

Megachurch pastor Joel Osteen once shared that he played basketball with a group of guys at a local club. They had no idea he was a preacher. He didn't announce it, he just lived out his faith. The other men always relied on him to make the call if there was a dispute, because they trusted him to be fair. It wasn't until much later that they saw him on television and realized he was a prominent preacher. They just knew he was a good guy, a man they could trust. Then they were much more ready to hear what he had to say about God, because they already knew him. They had already seen his integrity and good sportsmanship firsthand.

There's too much pressure in trying to be super-spiritual all the time. And, ultimately, you will accomplish the exact opposite of your goal. People will be turned off instead of drawn to you and your God.

A wonderful old church camp song says, "They will know we are Christians by our love." In other words, you don't have to shout the fact that you're a Christian. Let your love walk do the talking. That will speak volumes to those around you. They will want to know your secret to happiness, and you will be ready to share!

UNEXPLAINABLE JOY

Who shall separate us from the love of Christ? Shall tribulation, or distress, or persecution, or famine, or nakedness, or peril, or sword?
ROMANS 8:35 NKJV

My neighbor Stephanie is an amazing woman. She runs a very successful business—as well as several marathons a year. She is a loving wife and mom. In addition, she and her husband, Ron, host a weekly prayer group at their home, and they are always quick to help anyone in their lives who might need assistance. Need someone to watch your children? Steph is on call. Need agreement in prayer about something? Call Steph. She is, without a doubt, a true example of the Proverbs 31 woman.

But my favorite thing about Steph is this: She is joyful no matter what. She isn't moved by circumstances. She is only moved by heaven. And when you are only moved by heaven, you can be at peace in all things.

Several years ago Steph and Ron walked through a tragedy that would shatter most people—the death of one of their twin daughters. They went to the hospital with twin toddlers, and they came home with Hannah and an empty car seat. Sarah had died following a surgery to repair her heart.

It was devastating.

Yes, there were times when Steph cried out to God, hurting so badly she didn't want to get out of bed. But, through this tragedy, a great testimony arose. She and Ron drew closer to God and to each other, and now they know God in a way they had never known Him before. They share their testimony whenever God opens that door, and they are quick to give God glory for allowing Sarah to be a part of their lives—no matter how short that time was here on earth.

Every time Hannah and Sarah's birthday rolls around, Steph is given an opportunity to dwell in sadness and heartache, but she doesn't. Tears come at times, but even then she has a peace and joy inside her that is unexplainable.

This kind of joy comes only from spending time in God's presence.

I pray that none of us will ever have to encounter a tragedy of this magnitude. But I also pray that if we do, we will follow Ron and Steph's lead and turn to the Father for comfort and an infusion of His super-natural joy.

There is nothing in your life—no matter how bad it seems—that God can't see you through. He is there, waiting to love you and heal your hurting heart. And He promises to give you His joy for the journey ahead.